JACKIE JOKES

THE
ULTIMATE
COLLECTION

Jackie Martling

FOREWORD BY PENN JILLETTE

Post Hill
PRESS

A POST HILL PRESS BOOK
ISBN: 978-1-68261-497-6
ISBN (eBook): 978-1-68261-498-3

Jackie Jokes:
The Ultimate Collection
© 2018 by Jackie Martling
All Rights Reserved

Cover art by Cody Corcoran
Cover Photography by Bob Carey

Post Hill Press
New York • Nashville
posthillpress.com

Published in the United States of America

Table of Contents

This book is dedicated to joke tellers everywhere.
Please don't ever stop...

Acknowledgments

I'd like to thank Penn Jillette for his great Foreword, the gang at Post Hill Press for unleashing this culmination of six decades of joke collection, my family and friends, my fans, the countless folks who have been listening to me tell these jokes forever, Oglio Records for releasing six CDs of them…and especially my wonderful girlfriend Barbara Klein, who somehow continues to laugh at them…

Foreword
by Penn Jillette

I'm going to write seriously about my friend, Jackie. It's the only serious thing you're going to get in this book. It's the only words you'll see about Jackie in this book. Jackie's subject is rarely Jackie, and that's what makes him so important. It's what makes me want to write seriously about him.

Modern American stand-up comedy starts with Lenny Bruce. Lenny Bruce helped pave the way for Jackie to write a book full of fuck, cunt, and shit. But Lenny also made Jackie rare and valuable. Lenny inspired comics to talk about themselves. From the middle of the twentieth century most comics talk about their own fucks, cunts, and shit. They talk about their own love lives, their own divorces, and their own drug addictions. Jokes changed from, "A guy walks into a bar" to, "I broke up by text with this guy while I was walking into a bar." Comedy changed from jokes we could all tell into funny observations we could all could relate to. Comedy went from "we" to "I."

I first got to know Jackie when I was doing Stern regularly in the '80s. Jackie was laughing like an idiot into the microphone and scribbling jokes in real time and handing them to Stern. Howard would read the Jackie jokes about all of us and blend them in real time with Howard's own personal jokes about Howard. Jackie kept

ix

laughing and scribbling. Howard was "I," Jackie was "we." Jackie made Howard even funnier and rescued him from solipsism.

I didn't see Jackie perform live until recently. I watched him work Vegas. He killed. People couldn't breathe. Jackie is funny and Jackie is skilled. Who cares? A lot of people are funny and skilled. What's important is that Jackie is documenting our culture. These are jokes that belong to all of us. Jackie's not trying to find something different—he's trying to find things that are the same. He unites us. Jackie isn't Bob Dylan creating something new out of our folk tradition. Jackie is Alan Lomax, collecting the folk music that our culture created together.

Jackie's telling our own jokes back to us. He knows more of them than anyone else and he tells them better than anyone else but the jokes belong to all of us. Jackie didn't write them, Jackie collected them and put them in their best form. Jackie's shows and books are the *Smithsonian's Folkways Records* of comedy. You want to see a genius talking about herself? Go see Amy Schumer. You want to learn about America? Go see Jackie.

There are a lot of geniuses in comedy. Maybe Jackie is one of them, but I can't type that seriously. Jackie loves to tell our jokes. These jokes belong to all of us. I'm glad we have Jackie to take care them.

Okay, enough serious bullshit. Let's get to the fucks, cunts, and shit we all created together.

Thank you, Jackie.

SECTION ONE

Old Faceful

A couple goes to the marriage counselor.

The marriage counselor says, "I think we should start with something you have in common."

The husband says, "Neither of us likes to suck cock."

||||||||||||||||||||||||||

A girl goes to the gynecologist and says, "Doc, I'm freaking out. I keep finding postage stamps from Costa Rica in my vagina."

He examines her says, "Lady, those aren't *postage stamps*—they're the stickers from bananas."

||||||||||||||||||||||||||

A guy wakes up in the hospital and a nurse standing over him says, "You've been in a very bad car accident. You won't be able to feel anything from the waist down."

He says, "So would it okay if I squeezed your tits?"

||||||||||||||||||||||||||

A lady walks into a drugstore and says, "I need to buy some cyanide to kill my husband."

The pharmacist says, "Lady, I can't sell you cyanide to kill your husband. You'll go to jail, I'll go to jail, you're crazy."

She reaches into her purse, pulls out a picture, and hands it to the pharmacist. It's a picture of her husband fucking the pharmacist's wife.

The pharmacist says, "You didn't tell me you had a *prescription*."

||||||||||||||||||||||||||

A golfer walks into the clubhouse and his face is all clawed up and bleeding.

The pro says, "What happened to *you?*"

He says, "I just blew an eagle."

|||||||||||||||||||||

How do you get a fat girl in bed?

Piece of cake.

|||||||||||||||||||||

Ferguson goes for skydiving lessons.

The instructor says, "It's very simple. You leap out of the plane and you pull the ripcord. If nothing happens, you pull the emergency cord. It's that easy."

Ferguson goes up in the plane, jumps out, and completely forgets.

All of a sudden, he passes another guy, who's coming *up...*

The hockey player says, "Hey, man...you know anything about *parachutes?*"

The other guy says, "No. You know how to light a *gas stove?*"

|||||||||||||||||||||

Mrs. Viatori says to her sister, "The Gay Pride Parade is today."

Her sister says, "We suck cock and take it in the ass. Why don't nobody never throw *us* a parade?"

|||||||||||||||||||||

A rancher says to his Mexican foreman, "I think sex is fifty percent work and fifty percent play. What do you think, José?"

José says, "I theenk sex, eet ees one hundrett percent play."

The rancher says, "Why's that?"

José says, "Because eef eet were any kinte off work, for sure you would make *mee* do eet."

||||||||||||||||||||||

Bergin calls the doctor.

He says, "Doc, you've got to come right over. I swallowed a fifty-cent piece two years ago."

The doctor says, "Why didn't you call me two years ago?"

Bergin says, "Two years ago I didn't need the money."

||||||||||||||||||||||

What's the difference between pussy and apple pie?

Everybody *loves to eat the crust on your Mom's apple pie.*

||||||||||||||||||||||

A girl says to her friend, "I'm going to ask my doctor how many calories there are in sperm."

Her friend says, "Why? If you're swallowing that much, nobody's going to give a fuck if you're a little chubby."

||||||||||||||||||||||

Oringer's golfing with his wife and they're just teeing off. She hits from the ladies' tee and then Oringer hits from the men's tee a few yards behind her. He slices it very low and way off to the right, it hits his wife in the back of the head, and she goes down like a sack of potatoes. She's out.

Oringer calls 911, they rush her to the Emergency Room, and

a few minutes later the doctor comes out and says to Oringer, "I'm, sorry, sir, but your wife died immediately from the impact of the ball on her head and brain. But what's really puzzling is I found a golf ball in her anal cavity."

Oringer says, "Oh, that was my Mulligan."

||||||||||||||||||||||

What's the difference between a poor marksman and a constipated owl?

A poor marksman shoots *and* shoots *and never hits.*

||||||||||||||||||||||

Jesus is on the cross with his disciples at his feet when suddenly he yanks one of his hands free.

He reaches for his cock, goes *"Ahhhh,"* and squirts jizz all over the followers at his feet.

After he's done unloading, one of the disciples says, "Jesus, I'm shocked that once your hand was free the first thing you did was jack off."

Jesus says, "Actually, I was reaching down to cover my naked prick and I forgot all about the hole in my hand."

||||||||||||||||||||||

What's the last line of the obituary of the world's angriest person?

In lieu of flowers, go fuck yourself.

||||||||||||||||||||||

A slice of pizza's in a stomach, waiting to be digested, when a shot of whiskey washes past him. A few minutes later, a double shot of whiskey goes by. A few minutes later, a shot of tequila goes by.

The piece of pizza says to the shot of tequila, "What's going on up there?"

The shot of tequila says, "They're having a really great party."

The piece of pizza says, "Oh, *yeah*? I think I'll go up and have a look."

||||||||||||||||||||||||||

Sheen's swerving down the road and gets pulled over.

The cop says, "You have to take a Breathalyzer test."

Sheen says, "I can't. I have asthma, and if I do that I'll have a big coughing fit."

The cop says, "Then I have to give you a blood test."

Sheen says, "You can't do that. I'm a hemophiliac, and if you prick me I'll bleed all over the place."

The cop says, "Then you have to get out of the car and walk a straight line."

Sheen says, "I can't do that."

The cop says, "Why not?"

Sheen says, "Because I'm *drunk*, you idiot. Didn't you see how I was driving?"

||||||||||||||||||||||||||

After a two-day bender, O'Rourke wakes up in a cemetery lying in a freshly dug grave.

He says, "I-if I'm alive, h-how come there's a tombstone? And i-if I'm dead, h-how come I have to take a piss?"

||||||||||||||||||||||||||

Hayman's walking along a cliff when he comes up to a girl standing on the edge.

He says, "What're you doing?"

She says, "I'm trying to get up the nerve to jump."

He says, "Hey, as long as you're gonna kill yourself anyway, how about you have sex with me first?"

She says, "You *jerk*! You *asshole*! *Get the fuck out of here.*"

He says, "Okay, I'll just meet you down at the bottom."

||||||||||||||||||||||

Kennedy's sitting in his favorite chair watching football on TV. His wife walks up behind him and *smacks!* him on the back of the head with an iron frying pan.

He says, "What was that for?"

She says, "I was doing the laundry and I found a piece of paper in your pocket that said Dorothy."

He says, "Well...I-I went to the track last week, and that was to remind me of the horse I wanted to bet on."

She says, "Oh."

A few days later, he's sitting in his favorite chair, watching football on TV. Same wife, same frying pan...She walks up behind him and *smacks!* him on the back of the head.

He says, "What was *that* for?"

She says, "Your horse just called."

||||||||||||||||||||||

Spinato starts a new job and the boss tells him, "If you marry my daughter, I'll make you a partner, give you an expense account, a Mercedes, and an annual salary of a million dollars."

Spinato says, "What's wrong with her?"

The boss shows him a picture. The girl's hideous...a real showstopper.

The boss says, "She's not only ugly, she's as dumb as a box of rocks."

Spinato says, "Then I don't care what you offer me; it ain't worth it."

The boss says, "Howsabout if I give you a five-million-dollar salary and build you a mansion on Long Island?"

Spinato takes the deal, figuring he can put a bag on her head when they have sex. About a year later, he buys an original van Gogh and he's hanging it on the wall.

He climbs the ladder and yells to his wife, "Bring me a hammer."

She mumbles, "Get the hammer, get the hammer," and she fetches the hammer.

Spinato says, "Now go and get me some nails."

She mumbles, "Get the nails, get the nails," and she gets him some nails.

Spinato starts hammering a nail into the wall, hits his thumb, and yells, "*Fuck.*"

She mumbles, "Get the bag, get the bag..."

||||||||||||||||||||||||||

Farmer Hoagland kisses his wife goodbye and takes off for the fields. A few minutes later, he realizes he forgot his lunch pail and goes home to get it. When he walks in the house, his wife is lying naked on the kitchen floor and the local dentist is standing there nude right next to her.

The dentist squats down and says, "I'm glad you're here, Hoagland. I was just telling your wife that if she doesn't pay your dental bill, I'm gonna shit all over the floor."

||||||||||||||||||||||||||

A couple's on vacation.

The husband goes up to a wishing well, throws in a penny, *ploop!*...and nothing.

The wife takes out a penny, walks up, trips ass-over-head, falls into the wishing well, and drowns.

He says, "*Fuck!* It *works!*"

|||||||||||||||||||||||||r

Harkaway's on vacation, all alone in the south of France, walking along the beach, when he sees a woman lying in the sand, and she has no arms or legs.

He walks up to her...on his own, obviously she couldn't wave him over...and when he gets close, she says, "Oh, monsieur, I have no never, no never been keeeesed. Can monsieur please geeev me zeee *keees*?"

He says to himself, "What the hell?" and he kisses her.

She says, "Oh, monsieur, I have not never had zeee fin*gare*... could you please geev me zeee fin*gare*?"

Harkaway sneaks his finger around the lip of her bathing suit and sticks it in her very greasy unused hole.

She says, "Oh, monsieur, I have never had zeee *fuck*."

Harkaway picks her up, throws her in the water, and says, "Oh, you're fucked now."

||||||||||||||||||||||||

Norris is in a hot air balloon, and he's lost over Canada. He looks down and sees a bunch of skaters on a pond playing ice hockey.

He shouts down, "Where am I?"

One of the hockey players yells back up, "You're in a *basket*, ya dumb shit."

Minervini's driving along doing fifty-five when his wife says, "I want a divorce."

Minervini takes the car up to seventy.

She says, "I've been fucking your best friend and he's got a much bigger cock than you."

Minervini takes the car up to eighty.

She says, "My lawyer told me I get the house and the kids."

Minervini steps on it and gets the car up to ninety.

She says, "I'm taking the car, the checking account, and all the credit cards."

As Minervini starts to steer towards a bridge piling, she says, "Is there anything *you* want?"

He says, "Nope. I've got everything I need."

She says, "What's left?"

He says, "I've got the fucking air bag."

IIIIIIIIIIIIIIIIIIIIIIII

Three cross-eyed criminals come up in front of a cross-eyed judge.

The judge says to the first prisoner, "What's your name?"

The second prisoner says, "Johnny Johnson."

The judge looks at him and says, "I wasn't talking to you."

The third prisoner says, "I didn't say anything."

IIIIIIIIIIIIIIIIIIIIIIII

A parrot's on a perch in front of a pet store when a lady comes walking by.

The parrot says, "Hey, *lady!*"

She says, "What?"

He says, "You're really fucking ugly."

She keeps walking. A few hours later she comes walking back down the sidewalk.

The parrot says, "Hey, *lady!*"

She says, "*What?*"

The parrot says, "You're *really fucking ugly.*"

She goes in and says to the pet store owner, "That parrot is so rude! He really upset me! I'm gonna sue you and I'm gonna *own* this pet store."

The pet store owner says, "Lady, lady, calm down, calm down. I'll talk to the parrot, and it'll never happen again."

The next day, the lady passes the parrot, and the parrot says, "Hey, *lady!*"

She says, "*What?*"

The parrot says, "You know."

||||||||||||||||||||||

Where do porn stars go to college?

Fuck U.

||||||||||||||||||||||

Farmer Schmitt has a group over to play poker and little Jethro keeps running around the table, yelling out loud what cards everybody's holding. No matter what the farmer gives his kid to do, he keeps coming back and wrecking the game.

Finally, Farmer Schmitt's neighbor says, "This here ain't no good. We're gonna get out of here."

Reverend Bates says, "Hold on," leads Jethro out of the room, and comes back in a few minutes later. And after that, they never see the kid again.

Farmer Schmitt says, "Rev, what the heck'd you do to Jethro?"

The reverend says, "I showed him how to jerk off."

||||||||||||||||||||||

Conklin's fucking his wife and he says, "Did I hurt you?"
She says, "No. Why do you ask?"
He says, "You *moved*."

||||||||||||||||||||||

The teacher's trying to get all of her students to buy a copy of
the class picture.
She says, "Just think how nice it will be to look at it when you're
all grown up. You'll say, 'There's Jessie, she's a social worker,' or,
'That's Michael, he's a priest.'"
Dirty Johnny yells out, "And there's the teacher. She's dead."

||||||||||||||||||||||

Bernie's on his death bed.
The doctor pulls his wife to the side and says, "It doesn't look
good. I don't expect him to make it to morning. Try to comfort him
as best you can."
She goes to him and says, "Bernie, it's bleak. The doctor says
you'll be dead and cold by morning. What can I do to make it better,
Bernie? What can I do to comfort you?"
Bernie says, "Sylvia, after I die, would you please marry Sol?"
She says, "But I thought you *hated* Sol."
He says, "I do."

||||||||||||||||||||||

A porn star moves to suburbia and he's mowing the lawn when
his neighbor comes out.
The porn star says, "Where're you going?"

12

His neighbor says, "I've got a blind date."

When he gets home a few hours later, the porn star's sitting on his front steps smoking a joint.

The porn star says, "How was it?"

The neighbor says, "I only got to first base."

The porn star says, "Well, at least you got your asshole licked."

JACQUE IXXES

SECTION TWO

Drop a Load in Fanny

Eddie stumbles in really late & really drunk. In the shadows, he sees his wife sleeping on the floor with her ass sticking out from under a blanket. He yanks off his pants and does her deep in the ass. When he's done, he walks into the bathroom, and there's his wife, sitting on the bowl, taking a dump.

He says, "Wh-what're you d-doing?"

She says, "What do you mean, *what am I doing?* I'm going to the bathroom."

Eddie says, "Then wh-who'd I just fuck on the, on the living room f-floor?"

She says, "*Mama!*" and she runs into the living room.

She says, "Mama, are you okay?"

Her mother says, "Of *course* I'm okay."

She says, "But Eddie just had sex with you! Why didn't you say something?"

Her mother says, "Listen, sweetie, I haven't spoken to that piece of shit in twenty years, and I wasn't about to start tonight."

|||||||||||||||||||||||

What's the difference between a man's legs and a woman's legs? *The same set of balls is always dangling between a man's legs.*

|||||||||||||||||||||||

Nelson's golfing in a new foursome with two guys and a girl. He slices a shot into the woods. She comes with him to look for it, offers him a blow job, and he, of course, accepts. Over the next few weeks the foursome play a bunch of times and each round Nelson purposely hits a ball into the woods, she follows, and he gets another blow job.

As he's pulling up his pants after his fourth blow job he says, "Why don't we go on a date so we don't have to do this on the sly?"

She says, "Well, I'm actually a female impersonator."

He says, "You piece of shit! And all this time you've been hitting from the red tees?"

||||||||||||||||||||||

Mittleman goes to the doctor and says, "Doc, I can't sleep, but I can't take pills either."

The doctor says, "No problem. I'll just put a sleeping pill in a suppository and you can take it anally."

The next day the doctor calls Mittleman and says, "Well? Did it work?"

Mittleman says, "It worked too good. I woke up with my finger in my asshole."

||||||||||||||||||||||

A blind guy goes into Macy's, walks out to the middle of the floor, picks up his seeing-eye dog by the tail, and starts twirling it over his head.

A salesman comes up and says, "Can I help you?"

The blind guy says, "Nah, I'm just looking around."

||||||||||||||||||||||

A princess is walking along when she looks down and sees an ugly frog.

She picks it up and says, "My, but you're an ugly frog."

The frog says, "Don't I know it, lady. I got a really bad spell put on me. I gotta tell you, it sucks looking like this."

The princess says, "You know, I've seen lots of frogs who've had spells cast on them, but none of them was as ugly as you."

The frog says, "Jesus *Christ*, honey, you don't have to beat it into the ground. I *told* you, it's a really bad spell."

She says, "If I kiss you, will you turn into a prince?"

The frog says, "My best guess is no. I'm thinking a spell this bad'll probably take a blow job."

|||||||||||||||||||||||

What's round, sits on a wall, and has a crack through it? *Humpty Cunt.*

|||||||||||||||||||||||

Two cops are going to schools giving anti-drug lectures, but only one of them is getting good results, so the lieutenant asks them to tell him about their speeches.

The not-so-successful cop draws a big circle and a little circle, and says, "I tell them the big circle is your brain and the little circle is your brain on drugs."

The successful cop draws a little circle and a big circle and says, "I tell them the little circle is your asshole and the big circle is your asshole in jail."

|||||||||||||||||||||||

Bomback says to his new psychiatrist, "I had a really weird dream last night. I was with my mother, but when she turned around, she had *your face*. It was very disturbing. In fact, it woke me up and I never got back to sleep. I just lay there waiting for morning to come. Then I got up, drank a Coke, and came right over here. Can you explain my dream?"

The psychiatrist says, "A *Coke?* You call *that* a *breakfast?*"

||||||||||||||||||||||

What's a fart?
A piece of shit honking for the right of way.

||||||||||||||||||||||

A girl goes up to a guy at the bar, puts her arm around him, and says, "Are you the manager?"

He says, "Yes, I am."

She starts running her fingers through his hair and says, "Is it your job to keep the customers *satisfied?*"

He says, "Y-yes, it is..."

She starts playing with his face, works two of her fingers around and into his mouth, he starts sucking them wildly, and she says, "Can I tell you a *dirty little secret?*"

He says, "*Mmm-hmm...mmm-hmm....*"

She says, "There's no toilet paper in the fucking Ladies Room."

||||||||||||||||||||||

Little Red Riding Hood's skipping down the road when she sees the Big Bad Wolf crouching down behind a log.

She says, "My, what big *eyes* you have," and the Big Bad Wolf jumps up and runs away.

A little farther down the road Little Red Riding Hood sees the Big Bad Wolf crouched down behind a bush.

She says, "My, what big *ears* you have," and the Big Bad Wolf jumps up and runs away again.

A few miles down the road Little Red Riding Hood sees the Big Bad Wolf crouched down behind a rock.

She says, "My, what big *teeth* you have."

The Big Bad Wolf jumps up and says, "Will you *knock it off?* I'm trying to take a shit."

|||||||||||||||||||||

What do me and the neighbor's three-year-old have in common?
We both want his mommy.

|||||||||||||||||||||

A Chinese lady goes to the eye doctor.
He examines her and says, "Lady, you've got a cataract."
She says, "No, I've got a Rincoln Continentoo."

|||||||||||||||||||||

Why do drunks puke in the gutter?
To piss off the other bowlers.

|||||||||||||||||||||

Pascucci, Goodstein, and Dumbrowski are talking about their daughters.

Pascucci says, "I was-a cleaning my daughter's room the other day and I-a found a pack of cigarettes. I didn't even know she's-a smoke-a."

Goodstein says, "That's *nothing*. I was cleaning my daughter's room the other day and I found a *full bottle* of *vodka*. I didn't even know she *drank*."

Dumbrowski says, "Hey, I was cleaning my daughter's room the other day and I found a box of rubbers. I didn't even know she had a cock."

|||||||||||||||||||||

Why'd my wife cross the road?
To get back to the shoe store we were in three fucking hours ago.

|||||||||||||||||||||||

Iacovelli's eating a bowl of soup in a restaurant when he gets up and leaves without paying. The owner follows him out the door and down the street. Iacovelli walks into a whorehouse, grabs a girl, and goes upstairs.

The owner walks in and asks the Madam where the guy who just came in is and she says, "Upstairs, first door on the right."

He walks into the room, and there's Iacovelli, going down on the hooker to beat the band.

The restaurant owner says, "Hey, you left my restaurant without paying for your soup."

Iacovelli says, "There was a hair in it. I ain't paying for that."

The restaurant owner says, "A *hair in it?* Look at you. You've got your face *buried* in hair."

Iacovelli says, "And if I come across a noodle in here, I ain't paying for *this* either."

|||||||||||||||||||||||

McBagel's in the barber chair after his honeymoon.

The barber says, "How was your honeymoon?"

McBagel says, "I did a lot of fishing. Lots of fishing. I love to fish."

The barber says, "Did you get any sex?"

McBagel says, "Couldn't. She's got gonorrhea. So I did a lot of fishing. I love to fish."

The barber says, "Well, did you get a few blow jobs?"

McBagel says, "Couldn't. She's got pyorrhea. But I didn't care. I did a lot of fishing. I love to fish."

The barber says, "You could have gotten some ass sex."

McBagel says, "Nope. She's got diarrhea."

The barber says, "Jesus. Why the hell did you *marry* her?"

McBagel says, "Well, she's got worms, and you know how I love to fish."

|||||||||||||||||||||||

DeBellis says to the vet, "Doc, you gotta help me. Every time my dog takes a shit, as soon as he's done he turns around and eats it."

The vet says, "Oh, that's simple."

He opens a drawer, takes out a vial, hands it to DeBellis, and says, "Just give your dog two of these pills every day."

DeBellis says, "What'll they do?"

"Make the shit taste bad."

|||||||||||||||||||||||

The boss hands his secretary a note: "I want to have sex with you. I'll make you a great deal…I'll throw a thousand dollars on the floor, and by the time you pick it up I'll be done."

She calls her boyfriend to see if she should do it, and he says, "Well, hell yes. But tell him *two* thousand. If you pick it up fast enough he won't even have enough time to pull down his pants."

After a half hour, he calls back and says, "*Well?* What happened?"

She says, "The old bastard threw down two grand in quarters. I'm still picking and he's still fucking."

|||||||||||||||||||||||

DiNapoli's wife says, "DiNapoli, why's the laptop all sticky?"

He says, "It's not what you think, it's ice cream."

She says, "How'd you manage to get it all over the laptop?"

21

He says, "Did you ever try to eat an ice cream cone while you're jerking off?"

|||||||||||||||||||||

Quinn buys a robot that slaps people if they lie. He decides to test it out, so he brings the family and the robot into the kitchen after they eat.

He says to his son, "What'd you do before dinner?"

His son says, "I did my homework," and the robot slaps the kid. The son says, "Okay, okay, I was at Paul's house watching a movie."

Quinn says, "What kind of movie?"

His son says, *Star Wars*, and the robot slaps the kid again.

The son says, "Okay, okay, we watched some porn."

Quinn says, "*Porn?* When I was your age, I didn't even know what porn was," and the robot slaps Quinn.

Quinn's wife says, "He's your son, all right," and the robot slaps her.

Jenkins has a wooden leg. He starts chatting up a girl on Match. com, never tells her about it, and they make a date. They go to dinner, have a few drinks, she likes him, and they wind up back at his apartment. They go into his bedroom, she gets undressed, and gets under the covers.

He shuts off the lights and says, "I have a surprise for you."

He takes off his wooden leg, gets under the covers, and puts her hand on the stump.

She says, "*Wow*, what a great surprise. Have you got AstroGlide? I bet I can take it all."

|||||||||||||||||||||

An engaged woman, a married woman, and a mistress decide that one night they're going to wear S&M-style leather, stilettos, and a mask over their eyes, and see what happens with their partners.

When they meet a few days later, the engaged woman says, "Last night, when my fiancé came home, I was wearing the leather, the stilettos, and the mask, he said, 'Wow...you're *incredible*. I love you,' and we made love all night long."

The mistress says, "Last night, when we met in his office, I was wearing leather, stilettos, a mask over my eyes, and a raincoat. When I opened the raincoat, he didn't say a word. He just grabbed me and we had wild sex all night."

The married woman says, "Last night I sent the kids to stay at my mother's, and then got myself into the leather, the stilettos, and the mask. My husband walked in from work, grabbed a beer out of the refrigerator and the remote control and said, 'What's for dinner, Batman?'"

|||||||||||||||||||||||

Did you hear about the gay midget?
He came out of the cupboard.

|||||||||||||||||||||||

A lawyer says to his partner, "Are you fucking the new secretary?"
The other lawyer says, "No."
He says, "Then *you* fire her."

|||||||||||||||||||||||

It's the top of the third inning, fifth game of the 1956 World Series, and Don Larsen's pitching a perfect game. He walks out to the pitcher's mound, he's ready to pitch, but he stares at home plate for a long time. Then he motions for the catcher, Yogi Berra, to come out to the mound.

When Yogi gets to the mound, Don says, "For Christ's sakes, Yogi, button up your fucking fly. I'm getting mixed signals."

||||||||||||||||||||||

It's very late and Mrs. Lombardi walks in a half-day early from being out of town. She runs right up the stairs, opens the door to her bedroom, and sticking out from under the blanket she sees four legs instead of two. She freaks out, reaches for a baseball bat, and starts clubbing the blanket as hard as she can. When she finally can't hold the bat any more, she throws it to the floor and goes down to the kitchen to get a drink. When she walks in, there's her husband at the table reading a magazine.

He says, "Wow, you're home early, huh? Your parents came for a surprise visit, so I let them have our bed."

||||||||||||||||||||||

What's the best thing about an old woman's vagina?
It's a vagina.

SECTION THREE

Bugs Funny

Sloman goes into a whorehouse and says, "I want a girl with crabs."

The Madame says, "Get the hell out of here, none of my girls have crabs."

After he leaves, Jena says, "Business is so slow that I'm going to go yell to that guy to come back. I'll tell him I have crabs."

She goes to the door and yells, "*Hey!* Come on back, pal. I've got crabs and I'll do you."

They go up and get it on, and when they're done, she feels a little bad, so she says, "I have to tell you something. I don't have crabs."

Sloman says, "Oh, yes you do."

||||||||||||||||||||||

Two janitors at a Russian power plant find a container at work. It's got a weird smell, and figuring it's cheap vodka, they drink it all.

In the middle of the night, Nikita answers the phone, and Igor says, "Nikita, you know what was in that container? Rocket fuel."

Nikita says, "It didn't affect me at all."

Igor says, "Maybe not yet. But don't fart...I'm calling you from Tokyo."

||||||||||||||||||||||

What would you call a cow's vagina?
A count.

||||||||||||||||||||||

An old Jewish guy's walking along in Miami when a hooker says, "Come on, Pops."

He says, "All right," they go to a room, he gives her fifty bucks, and they have sex.

A few weeks after he gets back to New York, he realizes she

gave him the crabs. The next winter, the old guy's walking along in Miami and runs into the same hooker.

He says to her, "What're you selling *this* year? *Cancer?*"

||||||||||||||||||||||||

A farmer says, "Doc, once in a while when I'm out in the field I get excited and feel like romancin', but by the time I get back to the house I lose the feelin'."

The doctor says, "Just take your shotgun out into the field with you. When you get the feeling, shoot off the gun and when your wife hears it she can come out to you."

A few months later, the doctor sees the farmer in town and says, "So how's the old sex life?"

The farmer says, "Oh, it was great for a while, Doc. Until huntin' season come

and she run herself to death."

||||||||||||||||||||||||

A kid looks at his mother coming out of the shower and says, "Hey, Ma, you sure are getting' fat."

She says, "Yes, John. You see, I'm pregnant. I have a baby growing in my belly."

He says, "What's growin' in your *ass?*"

||||||||||||||||||||||||

A truck driver sees a girl about to jump off a bridge.

He stops, gets out, goes up to her, and says, "What are you doing?"

She says, "I'm going to commit suicide. My parents both hate me."

He says, "Well, before you jump, why not jump in the cab of my truck and give me a blow job?"

She's so forlorn, she figures what the hell. They hop in the cab of the truck, she sucks his dick, and takes down the whole charge with a huge *glurrppp!*

The trucker says, "*Man.* Now that's *talent.* I sure hate to see it go to waste like this. Why do your parents hate you?"

She says, "They're ashamed that I'm always dressing up like a girl."

‖‖‖‖‖‖‖‖‖‖‖‖‖‖‖‖

The Chinese waiter says, "Ah, mistah, you rike-a dinner?"

The husband says, "The duck was very rubbery."

The waiter says, "Ah, sank you velly much, and your wife, she velly rubbery too."

‖‖‖‖‖‖‖‖‖‖‖‖‖‖‖‖

Murphy dies, and at the funeral, his widow's standing at his casket as everybody passes by.

One neighbor says, "It's a shame Murphy's gone."

Mrs. Murphy says, "Yeah, 'tis a pity. Died of gonorrhea."

Her son is right next to her and he looks over at her.

The next guy passing by says, "I'm sorry Murphy's passed on."

Mrs. Murphy says, "Thank you. Yeah, taken by gonorrhea."

Her son pulls her aside and says, "Ma, Pop didn't die of gonorrhea. He died of *diarrhea.*"

She says, "Yeah, I know. But I'd much rather have them think that he went out as a *sport*, rather than the shit that he was."

‖‖‖‖‖‖‖‖‖‖‖‖‖‖‖‖

Why do cannibals like pregnant women?

There's a surprise inside.

|||||||||||||||||||||

Gallo walks his date home after their date.

When they reach the front door, he leans up against the house with one hand and says to her, "How about a blow job?"

She says, "Are you *crazy*?"

He says, "Don't worry, it'd be quick."

She says, "*No*. Somebody might see us."

He says, "Come on, suck my cock...you know how much you love to do it."

She says, "*No!* I said *no!*"

He says, "Come on, sweetheart..."

All of a sudden the girl's younger sister comes to the door in her nightgown, rubbing her eyes, and says, "Daddy says either *you* blow him, *I* blow him, or he'll come downstairs and blow the guy *himself*, but for Christ's sake tell this guy to take his hand off the fucking intercom."

|||||||||||||||||||||

At a big wedding reception, the bandleader says, "Okay, I want all of you married men to please stand next to the person who has made your life worth living."

The bartender gets crushed to death.

|||||||||||||||||||||

There's a knock on the door and when Moller answers it, he looks down and there's a snail looking up at him. He *kicks* the snail as far as he can.

Two years later, there's another knock on the door. Moller answers it, and there's the snail.

The snail looks up and says, "What the fuck was *that* all about?"

||||||||||||||||||||||||

Goldberger says to his wife, "I'm going to shoot my jizz in your ear."

She says, "No, don't, I might go deaf."

He says, "I doubt it. I'm always unloading in your mouth and you never shut the fuck up."

||||||||||||||||||||||||

The surgeon walks into Fugelsang's room and says, "Mr. Fugelsang, I have some good news and some bad news."

Fugelsang says, "What's the bad news, Doc?"

The surgeon says, "I accidentally cut off your penis."

Fugelsang says, "*Jesus*, Doc! What's the *good* news?"

The surgeon says, "It wasn't malignant."

||||||||||||||||||||||||

Farrington goes to the Post Office to apply for a job and the interviewer says, "Were you in the service?"

Farrington says, "Yeah, I did three tours in Iraq."

The interviewer says, "Are you disabled?"

Farrington says, "Yeah, a mortar round exploded near me and blew my testicles off. I'm on a hundred percent disability."

The interviewer says, "Okay, you're hired. The hours are eight to four, and you can start tomorrow. Come in at ten o'clock."

Farrington says, "If the hours are eight to four, why do you want me to come in at ten?"

The interviewer says, "This is a government job. For the first two hours we just sit around scratching our balls. No point in you coming in for that."

||||||||||||||||||||

A kid's in a confessional.

He says, "Bless me, Father, for I have sinned. I was thinking about my sister while I was masturbating."

The priest says, "That's a sin, all right. You've got two gorgeous brothers."

||||||||||||||||||||

An old guy in a retirement village knocks on his ex-wife's door.

She answers and he says, "M-my clothes are all dirty. W-wash them for me, w-will you?"

She says, "We're not married anymore. Get the fuck out of my sight."

A week later, he shows up again and says, "I-I'm hungry, can you fix me s-something to eat?"

She says, "We're not married anymore. Stay the fuck out of my sight."

A week later, he shows up and says, "I-I haven't got laid in a long t-time. Can we do it, j-just once?"

She says: "Okay, just once. And only from behind."

He says, "Wh-why from behind?"

She says, *"I want you the fuck out of my sight."*

||||||||||||||||||||

How many successful jumps do you need to join the Skydiver's Association?

All of them.

||||||||||||||||||||

A lady goes for her first golf lesson.

The pro says, "You've got to hold the club like you hold your husband's organ."

The lady takes the club and hits the ball.

He says, "Beautiful. Perfect shot. Right down the fairway. Now, take the club out of your mouth, put it in your hands, and we'll go for distance."

|||||||||||||||||||||

Sabean's on the road and doesn't realize he's gone into a bar full of transvestites. He starts talking to a good-looking...ahem... *woman*...and they really hit it off. They have a few drinks and then they leave the bar and climb into the back seat of his car.

After a few minutes, he says, "Are you pregnant?"

She says, "*Umm*...um, yes. Yes, I am."

He says, "I thought so. The kid's arm is hanging out."

|||||||||||||||||||||

McDonald goes to Hell and he's met by the Devil.

The Devil says, "The punishments are changed every thousand years. You have your choice of three rooms."

The first room has a young guy strapped to a pole being whipped. The next room has a middle-aged guy being tortured with fire. The third room has an old guy chained to the wall getting a blow job from a pretty blonde.

McDonald says, "I'll take the third room."

The Devil taps the blonde on the shoulder and says, "Okay, Miss, you can stop. This guy's replacing you."

|||||||||||||||||||||

A lawyer parks his brand-new Lexus in front of his office, and as he gets out, a truck passes too close and completely tears off the door on the driver's side.

When a cop pulls up, the lawyer's screaming, "My *Lexus!* My Lexus is ruined! It'll never be the same! *It'll never be the same!*"

The cop shakes his head in disgust, and says, "I can't believe how materialistic you lawyers are. You're so focused on your possessions that you don't notice anything else. You don't even realize that your left arm is missing from the elbow down. It must have been torn off when the truck hit you."

The lawyer says, "*Fuck!* Where's my *Rolex?*"

||||||||||||||||||||||||

What're two words you don't want to hear when you're standing at a public urinal?

Nice cock.

||||||||||||||||||||||||

A little girl comes home from school and says, "Ma, is it true that babies come out boys where put their wieners in?"

Her mother says, "Yep."

The girl says, "Won't that knock my teeth out?"

||||||||||||||||||||||||

Dirty Johnny's mother's making stew and accidentally drops in a packet of BBs.

The next day, Johnny sister comes down the stairs and says, "Ma, I was just doing a number two and there were BBs in it."

Her mother says, "Don't worry, honey, they'll just pass through you."

Johnny comes walking down the stairs and says, "Ma..."

His mother says, "I know, son. You were doing number two and there were BBs in it."

He says, "No. I was jerkin' off and I just shot the dog."

||||||||||||||||||||||||

A guy's girlfriend has a very small apartment, so she has a very small couch. She also has a cat, and the cat's always on the couch. Whenever he comes over and wants to sit down, he has to shoo the cat because there's no room for both of them on the couch. *Every time* he has to shoo the cat off the couch, so eventually he hates the cat.

One day he goes to her apartment and she's not there. He puts the cat in his car, drives five miles, and lets the cat out of the car. When he gets back to the apartment, the cat's on the couch.

A few days later he goes to the apartment and she's not there, so he takes the cat, drives twenty miles, and lets the cat out of the car. When he gets back to the apartment, the cat's on the couch.

A few days later he goes to the apartment, and she's not there, so he takes the cat and drives a hundred miles. He goes over a river, into a city, drives thirty blocks, turns left, goes thirty more blocks, opens the window, tosses the cat out of the car, and *zooms!* back.

An hour and a half later he calls the apartment and his girlfriend answers.

He says, "Is the cat there?"

She says, "Yeah, he's on the couch."

He says, "Put him on the phone. I'm lost."

SECTION FOUR

The Deadliest Snatch

A lady gets out of the shower, slips and falls, and lands spread-eagled on the floor. She lands so hard that a vacuum's created in her pussy and she gets stuck. Her husband tries to pull her up but she won't budge. He pushes her shoulders *back...and forth...*but it's like she's glued there. He goes next door and gets the neighbor, and then both of them pull and pull, and rock her *back...and forth...*but she just won't budge.

The neighbor says, "Hey, I'll just go get my hammer and we'll bust up the tiles up around the insides of her thighs. That'll break the suction and then we can lift her up."

The husband says, "That's a good idea. But first let me twist her nipples a little and get her aroused."

The neighbor says, "Why in hell would you do *that?*"

He says, "I want to get her lubed up so we can slide her into the kitchen where the tiles are cheaper."

||||||||||||||||||||||

What has four legs and one arm?
A happy pit bull.

||||||||||||||||||||||

A girl's sitting at the bar drinking next to a blonde.
She says, "I slept with a Brazilian last night."
The blonde says, "*Ooo*, your *poor cunt*. How many is a brazillion?"

||||||||||||||||||||||

A drunk stumbles out of a bar with his car keys dangling in his hand and he bumps into a cop.
The cop says, "What're you doing?"
The drunk says, "S-somebody stole my car. I-it was right here at the end of this key."

The cop says, "Your zipper's open and your dick's hanging out."
The drunk looks down and says, "F-fuck, they g-got my girl too."

|||||||||||||||||||||

Mrs. Fecalburger walks into the delivery room just after her son's wife's given birth to their first baby.

Mrs. Fecalburger says to the brand-new mom, "I don't mean to be rude, but that child doesn't look anything like my son."

Her daughter-in-law pulls up her maternity gown and says, "I don't mean to be rude, either, but this is a *cunt*, not a fucking copy machine."

|||||||||||||||||||||

Teach a man to build a fire and he'll be warm all night.
Set a man on fire and he'll be warm for the rest of his life.

|||||||||||||||||||||

DePace is sitting at the bar and says to the bartender, "Bartender, who'd you vote for in the last election?"

The bartender says, "It's none of your business, Mac. Hey...don't you know you don't never talk politics in a bar?"

A few minutes later, DePace says, "Excuse me, bartender, but what church do you go to?"

The bartender says, "Once again, needledick, it's none of your business. And you should know you don't never talk religion in a bar, either."

A few minutes later, DePace says, "Hey...can I talk about sex?"

The bartender says, "Sure. Sure, pal. Sex is a *great* topic for barroom conversation."

DePace says, "*Fuck you.*"

|||||||||||||||||||||||||

What's easier to pick up the heavier it gets?
A woman.

|||||||||||||||||||||||||

Madonna says to her doctor, "Doc, I got a new boyfriend and he's only twenty. I want you to operate on me to make my pussy smaller, tight as a sixteen-year-old. And this's gotta be *our* secret, Doc...no leaks, no tabloids."

When she wakes up after the operation the doctor's standing there. She looks down at the foot of the bed and sees three bouquets of flowers.

She says, "Jesus *Christ*, how the fuck could you do this to me? I told you this was just between you and me."

The doctor says, "Maddie, Maddie, calm down. That first bouquet is from me. The second bouquet is from the anesthesiologist who works side-by-side with me, he's gay and he's one of your biggest fans...he won't tell a soul. And the third bouquet is from a guy in the burn unit who wanted to thank you for his new ears."

|||||||||||||||||||||||||

What's the best thing about having sex with yourself?
When you want a thumb up your ass, you don't have to ask.

|||||||||||||||||||||||||

An ant comes walking into a bar and he looks ragged.

The bartender says, "What happened to you?"

The ant says, "I just had a date with a giraffe, and between the fucking and the kissing, I'm *exhausted*."

|||||||||||||||||||||||

A high school couple's in the movies.
The girl says, "Jimmy, I think I swallowed your gum."
He says, "Nah, I was just clearing my throat."

|||||||||||||||||||||||

A lady says, "Doc, kiss me."
He says, "I can't."
She says, "Doc, please kiss me."
He says, "I can't."
She says, "Doc, *please* kiss me..."
He says, "Look, lady, I probably shouldn't even be *fucking* you."

|||||||||||||||||||||||

A midget's walking along and a beautiful girl's walking the other way.
He says, "Hey, what do you say to a little fuck?"
She says, "Hello, you little fuck."

|||||||||||||||||||||||

What's red and pink and slowly gets smaller in the middle of the kitchen?
A baby combing his hair with a potato peeler.

|||||||||||||||||||||||

Norton says, "Doc, I think I've got a sex problem. I can't get it up for my wife anymore."
The doctor says, "Come back tomorrow and bring her with you."

The next day, Norton shows up with his wife.

The doctor says to Norton's wife, "Please take off your clothes and lie on the table."

She does it, and then the doctor walks around the table a few times, looking her up and down.

The doctor pulls Norton to the side and says, "You're fine. She doesn't give me a hard-on either."

|||||||||||||||||||||||

Eagel's wife's constantly nagging him about his past.

Night after night, she says, "Come on, tell me, how many women have you slept with?"

Finally one night he says, "Okay, okay, I'll count them. One... two...three...four...you...six...seven..."

|||||||||||||||||||||||

Dalton's eating in a restaurant when he spots a gorgeous woman sitting all alone.

He calls over his waiter and says, "Please send that woman a bottle of your most expensive champagne on me."

The waiter quickly brings the champagne over to the woman, and says, "Ma'am, this is from the gentleman over there."

She says to the waiter, "Please tell him that for me to accept this champagne, he better have a Mercedes in his garage, a million dollars in the bank, and eight inches in his pants."

The waiter delivers the message and Dalton says, "Please go back and tell her I have *two* Mercedes in my garage, *three* million dollars in the bank, but I haven't even met her yet...so why in fuck would I cut off four inches?"

|||||||||||||||||||||||

Harry's selling his talking dog, a guy comes to buy it, and the guy says, "How much?"

Harry says, "Five thousand dollars."

The guy says, "For five thousand dollars, I want a demonstration."

Harry says, "No problem. Fido, what's on top of a house?"

Fido goes, "*Rrrr-roof.*"

The guy says, "Wait a minute..."

Harry says, "Wait a minute, wait a minute, the demonstration's not over. Fido, what's it feel like when you sit on sandpaper?"

Fido goes, "*Rrrr-ruff.*"

The guy turns to leave and says, "This is ridiculous."

Harry says, "Wait a minute, wait a minute, we're not done here. Fido, who was the greatest Yankee ballplayer of all time?"

Fido goes, "*Rrrr-Ruuth.*"

The guy says, "This is bullshit. See you later," and he storms out.

Fido looks up at Harry and says, "So who was it? Fuckin' *DiMaggio?*"

|||||||||||||||||||||||

Dirty Johnny walks past his parents' bedroom and he sees his mother bent over her dresser with his father fucking her from behind. His father looks over, sees Johnny, smiles, and winks at him.

When his father's finished, he walks past Johnny's room and sees Grandma bent over the dresser, with Johnny furiously fucking her from behind.

His father says, "Johnny, what're you *doing?*"

Johnny says, "Not so funny when it's *your* mother, eh, Pop?"

|||||||||||||||||||||||

A little girl's in school taking a true-false test and she's flipping a coin. At the end of the test, she's flipping the coin again.

The teacher says, "What're you doing?"

She says, "Checking my answers."

||||||||||||||||||||

Elder walks into a costume party stark naked except for a pair of roller skates.

The host says, "What are you supposed to be?"

He says, "A pull toy."

||||||||||||||||||||||||

It's harvest time and the old Italian farmer and his teenage daughter load all the vegetables onto their horse-drawn wagon, go to town, sell them, and are on their way home when bandits come riding up, shooting their guns in the air.

The farmer is holding a huge wad of bills, and he says, "Oh, no...I'm-a work so hard, and now they-a gonna take-a all my money. Oh, Maria, what I-a gonna do?"

Maria says, "Papa, give me the money."

He hands her the wad of bills, she takes it, turns away from him, lifts up her dress, and *stuffs* it up inside her twat. The bandits stop the wagon and make the farmer and his daughter get down. They search them and the wagon, but they don't find anything. Mad as hell, they take off with the wagon and the horses.

The Italian farmer is crying his eyes out, and he says, "I'm-a work so hard, now we lose-a everything."

Maria says, "Papa, don't-a cry. I save-a the money."

She lifts up her dress and *slurrp!* pulls the wad of bills out of her snatch.

The farmer says, "Oh, Maria! *Maria!* You save-a the money! I'm-a so happy!"

Then he thinks a second and starts to cry again.

Maria says, "Papa! I save-a the money! Why you cry now?"

The farmer says, "Maria, if we had-a brought your Mama, we could-a saved-a the wagon and-a the horses."

||||||||||||||||||||||

After seven years in jail, Ratcliffe's sentence is finally up, so his wife and his son go to pick him up at the prison.

He comes out through the barred doors, looks at his wife, and says, "F. F."

She says, "E. F."

As they're walking out to the car, he says, "F. F."

She says, "E. F."

They get in the car, and he says, "F. F."

She says, "E. F."

The kid says, "Pop, what's goin' on?"

Ratcliffe says, "Your mother wants to *eat* first."

||||||||||||||||||||||

Two hippies are standing on a boardwalk looking out at the ocean.

The first one says, "*Man*...look at all that *water*, man."

The second hippie says, "Yeah...and that's just the *top*."

||||||||||||||||||||||

Two gay guys live together and it's one guy's birthday. The other guy goes out and buys a dozen prophylactics, fills them with Kool-Aid, and puts them in the freezer.

The birthday boy comes home and his friend says, "Surprise in the freezer! *Surprise in the freezer!*"

The birthday boy opens the freezer door, takes a look, and says, "My favorite! *Cocksicles!*"

|||||||||||||||||||||||||

The hockey coach pulls one of his seven-year-old players to the side of the rink and says, "Do you understand what cooperation is? What a *team* is?"

The kid says, "Yeah."

The hockey coach says, "Do you understand that what matters is not whether we win or lose, but how we play together as a unit?"

The kid says, "Yes, sir."

The coach says, "And I'm sure you know that when a penalty's called, you shouldn't argue and curse and spit on the referee and call him a cock-sucking moron, right?"

The kid says, "Right."

He says, "And when I call you off the ice so that another boy can get a chance to play, it's not good sportsmanship to call your coach a stupid piece of low shit, is it?"

The kid says, "Of *course* not."

The coach says, "Good. Now please go over there and explain all that to your mother."

|||||||||||||||||||||||||

A congregation honors a rabbi for twenty-five years of service by sending him to Hawaii for a week, all expenses paid. When the rabbi walks into his Kauai hotel room, there's a nude girl lying on the bed.

He picks up the phone, calls his temple, and says, "Where is your *respect*? As your rabbi, I am *very*, very upset," and he *slams!* down the phone.

The girl gets up and starts to get dressed.

He says, "Where are you *going*? I'm not angry at *you.*"

|||||||||||||||||||||||

The judge says to a double-homicide defendant, "Mr. Ravioli, you're charged with beating your wife to death with a hammer."

A voice at the back of the courtroom yells out, "You *bastard*."

The judge says, "You're also charged with beating your mother-in-law to death with a hammer."

The voice in the back of the courtroom yells out, "You *motherfucker*."

The judge stops the proceedings and says to the guy in the back of the courtroom, "Sir, I can understand your anger and frustration at this crime. But no more outbursts from you, or I'll charge you with contempt. Understand?"

The guy stands up and says, "Your honor, for fifteen years I've lived next door to that piece of shit, and every time I asked to borrow a hammer, he said he didn't have one."

|||||||||||||||||||||||

A little Jewish kid's walking past his parents' bedroom, the door's open, he looks in, and he sees his father naked on top of his mother.

He says, "What's going on, Papa?"

His father says, "We're making children."

The next night the kid's walking past his parents' bedroom, the door's open, he looks in, and he sees his mother sucking his father's cock.

He says, "What's going on, Mama?"

His mother says, "We're making *jewelry*."

|||||||||||||||||||||||

Schmidlap, Stukowski, and Washington are arguing about who has the biggest dick. They go out on the Observation Deck of the Empire State Building and hang them over.

Schmidlap says, "Check it out. This beauty reaches down to the sixty-eighth floor."

Stukowski says, "That's nothin'. This baby's danglin' down past the *thirty-fourth* floor."

They look over and they see Washington doing a jig, jumping back and forth.

Schmidlap yells over, "What the hell are you doing?"

Washington says, "Dodgin' traffic."

SECTION FIVE

North Polish Jokes

Three guys are drunk at a party on Christmas Eve. As they're leaving, they slip on the ice at the top of the stairs and they all fall to their deaths.

They come up to St. Peter and he says, "I'll tell you what, fellas. It's Christmas Eve. If you can do something to commemorate Christmas, I'll let you into Heaven."

The first guy reaches into his pocket, pulls out his lighter, flicks it on, and says, "A candle."

St. Peter says, "Excellent. Come in."

The second guy reaches into his pocket, pulls out his car keys, jingles them, and says, "Sleigh bells."

St. Peter says, "Creative. Come in."

The third guy reaches in his pocket, pulls out a pair of stained women's panties, puts them under St. Peter's nose, and says, "These are Carol's."

|||||||||||||||||||||||||||

A priest and a rabbi are walking down the street together and they both want a drink, but they have no money on them.

The priest says, "I've got an idea how to get us some free drinks."

He walks into a crowded bar alone and the rabbi stands at the door and watches. The priest orders a drink, downs it and then the bartender gives him his tab.

The priest says, "But my son, I've already paid for the drink."

The bartender says, "I'm terribly sorry, Father, but it's really busy in here and I must have forgotten."

The rabbi walks in and orders a drink.

After he downs it, the bartender gives him the tab and the rabbi says, "Son, I paid you when I ordered the drink."

The bartender says, "I'm terribly sorry, sir, I don't know what's wrong with me. That's the second time that happened to me tonight."

The rabbi says, "That's okay, son, no offense taken. Now, just give me change for the fifty I gave you and I'll be on my way."

||||||||||||||||||||||

Dirty Johnny's sitting on a park bench eating one candy bar after another.

After about the sixth one, a cop who's been watching him says, "Hey, kid, don't you know eating all that candy isn't good for you? It'll give you acne, rot your teeth, and make you fat."

Johnny says, "My grandfather lived to be a hundred and seven years old."

The cop says, "Did your grandfather eat that much candy?"

Johnny says, "No, he minded his own fucking business."

||||||||||||||||||||||

Davis says to his wife, "Honey, I think you should go bra-less."

She says, "Really? Do you think my breasts are still perky enough?"

He says, "No, but maybe it'd pull the wrinkles out of your face."

||||||||||||||||||||||

What's the difference between monkeys and midgets?
Monkeys don't freak me out.

||||||||||||||||||||||

Mercadante's in his car with a girl and says, "How about a hand job?"

She says, "I don't know what that is."

He says, "Remember when you were a kid and you used to shake up a Coke bottle and spray your brother with it? Just do that."

She says, "Okay."

He takes it out and she grabs it. A few minutes later, he starts screaming.

She says, "What's the matter?"

He says, "*Take your fucking thumb off the end.*"

|||||||||||||||||||||||

When's the worst time to drink diarrhea?

Anytime.

|||||||||||||||||||||||

Bergmann's an ad executive, he starts at a new company, and his first assignment is to come up with a billboard campaign for Johnson's Nails. A few weeks later, he brings his boss and the other top people into the boardroom to see his masterpiece, and he pulls the sheet off a billboard.

On the left, there's Jesus on the cross, and on the right it says, "We used Johnson's Nails."

The boss freaks out and says, "You *idiot!* That's *blasphemous!* The Christians would go *berserk!* We'd get tarred and feathered! We can't use that! You're a moron! You're *fired!*"

Bergmann says, "Give me another chance, give me another chance."

A few days later, Bergmann brings the boss and his co-workers in to see his new masterpiece and pulls the sheet off the billboard.

On the left, there's a cross, with nobody on it. On the right, Jesus is running, the Roman soldiers are chasing him, and one of the soldiers is looking out, yelling, "*We should have used Johnson's Nails.*"

|||||||||||||||||||||||

Reese goes up to a hooker and says, "How much for a blow job?"
She says, "A hundred bucks."
He says, "Okay," and he starts to jack off.
She says, "What're you *doing?*"
He says, "For a hundred bucks, you didn't think I was gonna give you the *easy* one, did you?"

|||||||||||||||||||||||

Eisner comes home from work and says to his wife, "I think one of the guys at work is a faggot."
She says, "Why do you think that?"
He says, "Today, we were standing at the urinals and he was jerking off."
She says, "How's that make him *gay?*"
He says, "He was using *my cock.*"

|||||||||||||||||||||||

An American woman and an Iranian woman are in the supermarket.
The Iranian woman picks up two potatoes and says, "These remind me of my husband's testicles."
The American woman says, "That big?"
The Iranian woman says, "No...that *dirty.*"

|||||||||||||||||||||||

What's the funniest thing in the world?
Ten blind guys trying to sit at a table set for eight.

||||||||||||||||||||||||

Peri decides to get artificially inseminated. She goes into the doctor's office and he starts taking off his clothes.

She says, "What are you *doing*?"

He says, "I'm all out of the bottled stuff...you're gonna have to settle for draft."

||||||||||||||||||||||||

Brrinngg!

The bell rings at the whorehouse. A girl answers the door, and there's a guy with no arms and no legs.

She says, "What do you think *you're* gonna do in here?"

He says, "I rang the bell, didn't I?"

||||||||||||||||||||||||

What's the difference between frustration and panic?

Frustration's the first time you find out you can't do it the second time...

Panic's the second time you find out you can't do it the first *time.*

||||||||||||||||||||||||

An eighty-year-old couple's having trouble remembering things so they go to see their doctor to make sure there's nothing wrong.

After he examines them, the doctor says, "You're both physically okay, but you guys might want to start writing notes to help you remember things."

That night they're watching TV when the old man gets up from his chair.

His wife says, "Where are you going?"

He says, "To the kitchen."

She says, "Will you get me some vanilla ice cream?"

He says, "All right."

She says, "Don't you think you should write it down?"

He says, "I don't have to write it down...vanilla ice cream."

She says, "Could I have strawberries and whipped cream?"

He says, "All right."

She says, "Don't you think you should write it down?"

He says, "I don't have to write it down...vanilla ice cream with strawberries and whipped cream."

Twenty minutes later he walks in and hands her a plate of bacon and eggs.

She says, "You forgot my fucking toast."

||||||||||||||||||||||||

A guy robs a bank and takes hostages.

He says to the first hostage, "Did you see me rob the bank?"

The hostage says, "Yeah," and the robber shoots him in the head.

The robber says to the second hostage, "Did you see me rob the bank?"

The guy points at the woman standing next to him and says, "No, but I'm pretty sure my wife did."

||||||||||||||||||||||||

Bangberger's kneeling in front of a headstone.

He's crying and saying, "If only you had lived, if only you had lived."

A gravedigger comes up to him and says, "Your wife's in there?"

Bangberger says, "No, my wife's first husband."

||||||||||||||||||||||||

An old woman's getting her portrait painted and she says to the artist, "I want you to paint a diamond and ruby tiara on my head, two big strands of pearls that hang to my waist around my neck, and two huge diamond earrings."

The painter says, "No problemo, lady. But why?"

She says, "My husband's fucking a young broad, and after I die, I want she should go crazy looking for the jewelry."

||||||||||||||||||||||

A girl calls up her mother and says, "Ma, I met this Greek guy, and I'm in love with him, and I'm gonna marry him."

Her mother says, "You wanna marry a Greek guy, that's fine with me. But whatever you do, don't let him flip you over."

She says, "All right, Ma."

About six months after they're married they're lying in bed one night and her husband says, "Honey, why don't you turn over?"

She says, "Oh, no. My mother told me never to turn over."

He says, "What, don't you wanna have any kids?"

||||||||||||||||||||||

A girl goes to the doctor and says, "Doc, I've got very small breasts. Can you help me?"

He says, "Sure. It's very simple. Every morning when you wake up, and every night before you go to bed, just massage your breasts for five minutes while you repeat this: 'Mary had a little lamb, its fleece was white as snow, and if I rub my boobs like this, surely they will grow.'"

The next morning, she's on the bus on her way to work when she realizes she forgot to do her exercises.

She goes to a seat in the back of the bus, turns to the window, and starts rubbing her boobs with both hands and saying, "Mary had a little lamb, its fleece was white as snow, and if..."

There's a tap on her shoulder. She turns and there's a guy standing there.

He says, "Excuse me, but do you go to Doctor Jason?"

She says, "Yeah. How did you know?"

He starts rubbing his crotch and says, "*Hickory dickory dock...*"

|||||||||||||||||||||||

Fraboni's smooching with his date when he tries to put his hand under her skirt.

She says, "Please don't. My mother made me promise never to let a man put his hand under my skirt. But if you put your hand down my back, it's the second hole you come to."

|||||||||||||||||||||||

Uchwat takes his wife out in his boat fishing. He drops anchor, reaches into a burlap sack, takes out a bullfrog, puts a stick of dynamite in its mouth, lights it, and throws it overboard. *Kaboom!* The dynamite goes off, and scads of fish are blown into the boat. Uchwat reaches into the sack, takes out another bullfrog, sticks a piece of dynamite in its mouth, lights it, and throws it off the other side of the boat. *Kaboom!* More fish are blown into the boat.

His wife says, "Honey, that isn't very sportsmanlike, is it?"

Uchwat reaches into his sack, takes out another bullfrog, sticks a piece of dynamite in its mouth, hands it to his wife, and says, "Are you gonna *talk*, or are you gonna *fish*?"

|||||||||||||||||||||||

Seefrantz is drinking at the bar when the fire whistle blows. He guzzles his drink and goes for his coat.

The bartender says, "I didn't know you were a volunteer fireman."

Seefrantz says, "I'm not. But my girlfriend's husband is."

||||||||||||||||||||

What's a snail?

A booger with a crash helmet.

||||||||||||||||||||

An Arab sheik says to an American tourist, "Mr. Schirippa, your wife, she is beautiful. I have to have her. I will trade you her weight in gold."

Schirippa says, "Give me a few days."

The sheik says, "To think it over?"

Schirippa says, "Hell, no. To fatten her up."

||||||||||||||||||||

The average vagina is eight inches deep, and the average penis is five and a half inches long...

Which means in New York City alone there's thirteen miles of unused pussy.

SECTION SIX
Roast Bestiality

What's the worst thing about fucking farm animals?
The next time you see them, they act like they don't even know you.

||||||||||||||||||||||

Sexton's friend's a pilot with a two-seater airplane. They go flying on a very nasty day, and just as they're flying into a really dark cloud, his friend slumps over dead of a heart attack.

Sexton pushes his friend out of the way, grabs the microphone, and says, "Mayday! *Mayday!* My friend the pilot just fell over dead. It's pitch black and we're flying upside-down."

The dispatcher says, "If it's pitch black, how do you know you're flying upside-down?"

He says, "Because there's shit oozing out of my shirt collar."

||||||||||||||||||||||

What do you call a kid with no arms and an eyepatch?
Names.

||||||||||||||||||||||

A missionary's in Africa and he gets caught by cannibals. They throw him into a bamboo jail and he sits there for two days.

Finally, one of the cannibals comes into the cell and says, "Have good news and have bad news. Good news, we not eat you. Bad news, Chief want have weenie roast."

||||||||||||||||||||||

A zebra gets loose from the zoo and finds his way to a farm.

He walks up to the hen and says, "What do you do around here?"

The hen says, "I lay eggs for the farmer."

He goes up to the cow and says, "What do you do around here?"

The cow says, "I give milk to the farmer."

The zebra goes up to the bull and says, "What do you do around here?"

The bull says, "You take off those faggot pajamas and I'll *show* you what I do around here."

‖‖‖‖‖‖‖‖‖‖‖‖‖‖‖‖‖‖‖

O'Neill goes into a men's room stall and sits down.

A guy in the next stall says, "How're you doing?"

O'Neill says, "Uh...fine."

The other guy says, "What a great day, huh?"

O'Neill says, "*Umm...yeah.*"

The other guy says, "Damn, I hope the Yankees win today. I've got a lot of

money on the game."

O'Neill says, "I-I don't bet."

The other guy says, "Listen, Don, I'll call you back later. Some jerk in the next stall keeps answering my questions."

‖‖‖‖‖‖‖‖‖‖‖‖‖‖‖‖‖‖‖

Caramico's out fishing way too long, he knows his wife is going to kill him and he's racing home over a bridge when a cop catches him on radar.

The cop walks up and Caramico says, "Please don't give me a ticket, I-I'm late for work."

The cop says, "What do you?"

Caramico says, "I'm a rectum stretcher."

The cop says. "A *rectum stretcher*? What's a rectum stretcher do?"

Caramico says, "Well, if they need me, they call and I go to their house. I start with a finger, then another finger, then the whole hand, then both hands. Then I *slowwwly* pull them apart, farther and farther, until they're a full six feet across."

The cop says, "What do you do with a six-foot asshole?"

Caramico says, "We give him a radar gun and stick him at the end of a fucking bridge."

||||||||||||||||||||||||||

A little kid's in the bathtub when his mother comes into the bathroom and undresses.

He points between her legs and says, "What's that, Mommy?"

She says, "*Umm*...that's where the Indian hit me with his tomahawk."

He says, "*Ouch*. Right in the cunt, eh?"

||||||||||||||||||||||||||

Lynch goes into a whorehouse and says to the madam, "I'm in the mood for something really different."

She says, "No problem. Alice, take this guy upstairs and sixty-nine with him."

The girl leads him upstairs into a room, they both get undressed, and she lies him down on the bed.

She's just going down on him and sticking it in his face when *llbbt*, she blasts a huge fart—cracks a rat right on his nose.

He pushes her off, gets up, and starts getting dressed.

She says, "What are you doing?"

He says, "I don't think I can handle sixty-eight more of those."

||||||||||||||||||||||||||

A guy stumbles into a bar and says, "B-bartender, g-gimme a beer."

The bartender says, "No booze for you, my friend. You're too drunk to even be in here."

The guy says, "I-I'm fine."

The bartender says, "I'll tell you what. Take this dart. If you can even hit that target on the wall, I'll give you a beer and a surprise."

The guy throws the dart and it hits dead center, a bullseye. So the bartender gives him a beer and hands him a box turtle somebody had brought in from the parking lot. A few hours later, the guy stumbles into the bar again.

He says, "B-bartender, g-gimme a beer."

The bartender says, "No way, pal, you're even drunker now."

The guy says, "I-I'm fine."

The bartender says, "Okay, take this dart again. If you can even hit that target on the wall, I'll give you another beer and another surprise."

The guy throws the dart and it hits dead center, another bullseye. The bartender gives him a beer and hands him a shiny new promotional corkscrew he had behind the bar.

The guy looks at the corkscrew and says, "I-I don't want this thing. G-gimme another ham on a hard roll."

|||||||||||||||||||||||

Bloom goes into a luncheonette and says to the girl behind the counter, "I want a bowl of hot chili."

She says, "I'm sorry, sir, the guy next to you got the last bowl."

He looks over and sees that the other guy's finished eating, but the chili bowl's still full.

He says, "Are you going to eat that?"

The other guy says, "No. You can have it, help yourself."

Bloom pulls it over and starts eating the chili. When he gets about half-way down, his fork hits a dead mouse.

He goes, "*Ugh!*" and pukes the chili back into the bowl.

The other guy says, "Yeah, that's about as far as I got too."

|||||||||||||||||||||||

What would you call a Jewish vagina?

A can't.

|||||||||||||||||||||||

Summers goes to his twentieth high school reunion and sees an old friend. The guy's wearing a three-corner hat, he's got a peg leg, a hook on his right hand, and a black patch over his left eye.

Summers says, "Robey, this is a *reunion*, not a costume party. What's up?"

Robey says, "Well, I always said I wanted to be a pirate, and now I am."

Summers says, "What happened to your leg?"

Robey says, "One day aboard ship during a battle, a cannonball blew off my left leg, so's I got me a peg leg."

Summers says, "How'd you wind up with a hook?"

Robey says, "A few weeks later, I got my right hand sliced off in a saber fight, so's I got me a hook."

Summers says, "And how'd you wind up with that patch?"

Robey says, "A bunch of seagulls were flying over us. I looked up and one of them shit in my eye."

Summers says, "A little bird shit shouldn't cause you to lose an eye."

Robey says, "First day with the hook."

|||||||||||||||||||||||

Spear and Travis are in a bar, drunk as skunks.

Spear says, "L-let's have one more drink and then go f-find some whores."

Travis says, "Nah, I've got more than I can handle at home."

Spear says, "Okay, then l-let's have one more drink and g-go to your place."

||||||||||||||||||||||

What are the two sides to every divorce?
Yours and shithead's.

||||||||||||||||||||||

Two drunks wake up one morning.

The first guy says, "H-how the hell are we gonna get drunk today? A-all I've got is f-forty cents."

The second guy says, "I've got an idea. Give me the money."

He goes into a delicatessen, comes out with a hot dog, and says to his friend, "Follow me."

They go to a bar and before they walk in, the second guy pulls down the first guy's zipper, puts in the hot dog, and then pulls the zipper back up enough to hold it.

They walk in and he says, "Bartender, two triple Jack Daniels."

The bartender gives them the drinks and they guzzle them down.

The bartender says, "Okay, pay up."

The second guy drops to his knees and starts sucking like mad on the hot dog.

The bartender says, "You fucking *homos!* Get the hell out of here."

Fifteen bars, they pull the same stunt. They're loaded to the gills.

The second guy says, "Wh-what an idea I had. Look at us,

b-bombed again, and it only cost us forty cents. B-but we've gotta stop. Every time I-I drop to my knees, they *smash* on the barroom floor. I-I can't take it anymore."

The first guy says, "Wh-what do you mean, *you* can't take it anymore? We lost the h-hot dog after the fourth b-bar."

|||||||||||||||||||||

A little old lady in a nursing home walks in front of an old guy sitting in the TV lounge, lifts up her nightie, and shouts, "*Su*-per pussy!"

He says, "Th-that pussy looked p-pretty, p-retty n-nasty. I-I'll take the soup."

|||||||||||||||||||||

Dirty Johnny walks into a whorehouse.

He says, "Hey, lady, I wanna catch V.D."

The madam says, "Kid, *why* would you want to catch V.D.?"

Johnny says, "Well, I figure if *I* get it, *I'll* give it to the *babysitter*, the *babysitter* will give it to my old *man*, my old man'll give it to the lady next *door*, and *she'll* give it to her *husband*. And *he's* the cocksucker who ran over my *bike*."

|||||||||||||||||||||

Merrill says to a psychiatrist, "Doc, every time I get in my bed, I think there's somebody under it. If I get under the bed, I think there's somebody on top of it. Top, under, top, under, you gotta help me, I'm losing it."

The doctor says, "You just need to put yourself in my hands. See me three times a week for two years and I'll cure all of your fears."

Merrill says, "How much do you charge?"

64

The doctor says, "Two hundred dollars per visit."

Merrill says, "I'll sleep on it."

Six months later Merrill runs into the doctor on the street.

The doctor says, "Why didn't you ever come to see me again?"

Merrill says, "For two hundred dollars a visit? A bartender cured me for ten bucks."

The doctor says, "Really. How?"

Merrill says "He told me to cut the legs off the fucking bed."

|||||||||||||||||||||

McEnery walks into a bar and orders three shots of whiskey. The bartender sets them up and McEnery drinks them down one after another. He does it at the same time every day for two weeks straight.

Finally, the bartender says, "Why do you always order three shots at a time?"

McEnery says, "I've got a brother in Poland and another brother in France. They do the same thing at the same time. It's like the three of us having a drink together every day."

The next day, McEnery walks into the bar and only orders two shots.

After he drinks them down, the bartender says, "What happened? Did one of your brothers die?"

McEnery says, "No. I quit drinking."

|||||||||||||||||||||

It's Friday afternoon, and a woman says to her neighbor over the fence, "Tom just called from work and told me he's gonna be bringing me home a dozen red roses. I guess I'll be spending the weekend on my back with my legs spread."

Her neighbor says, "Haven't you got a *vase*?"

|||||||||||||||||||||||||

The teacher says to her fourth grader class, "Try to imagine how the Indians must have felt when they first encountered the Spanish explorers. How would you feel if someone showed up on your doorstep who looked very different, spoke a strange language, and wore unusual clothes? Wouldn't you be a bit scared?"

Dirty Johnny says, "Nah, I'd just figure it was one my sister's dates. She'll fuck *anybody*."

|||||||||||||||||||||||||

What do you do if you're swallowed by a whale?
You run around until you get pooped out.

|||||||||||||||||||||||||

Meganck gets in bed with his wife.

He says, "Hey, babe, how about it?"

She says, "Not tonight, I've got a headache."

The next night they're in bed, and he says, "Hey, how about it?"

She says, "Not tonight, I'm too tired."

The next night the guy gets in bed and says, "Well, how about it?"

She pushes him away and says, "*Three nights in a row?* What are you, a *sex maniac?*"

|||||||||||||||||||||||||

One sperm says to the other sperm, "How far is it to the ovary?"

The other sperm says, "Relax. We haven't even passed the *tonsils* yet."

|||||||||||||||||||||||||

Three Polish kids flunk sex ed.
The first kid says, "We gotta get that bitch back."
The second kid says, "Yeah. We'll strip her."
The third kid says, "Yeah. And then we'll tie her up."
The first kid says, "Yeah. And then we'll suck her cock."

SECTION SEVEN

Funny the Pooh

Horace is walking along the sidewalk, grunting and moaning, "Uhh! *Ohh!* Unh..."

He passes a friend who's sitting on a stoop and his friend says, "Horace, what's wrong?"

Horace says, "Unh! *Ohh!* I shit my pants. *Unh...*"

His friend says, "Horace, if you shit your pants, why don't you go home and *change?*"

Horace says, "Unh! *Ohh!* Because I...I'm not finished yet. *Unh...*"

|||||||||||||||||||||||

A woman says to her doctor, "I have diarrhea. Can I take a bath?"

He says, "If you've got enough."

|||||||||||||||||||||||

The pilot comes on the intercom and says, "Thank you for flying West Eastern. We'll be touching down in Los Angeles in about five and a half hours. We appreciate your business."

He forgets to turn off the intercom, turns to the co-pilot, and says, "I think I'm going to go take a shit and then get a blow job from that hot new blonde stewardess."

The stewardess is in the back of the plane, realizes the intercom's still on, and goes running up the aisle to tell him.

A little old lady says, "Take your time, honey. He said he had to take a shit first."

|||||||||||||||||||||||

Crane says to his wife, "Look at this black golf ball. It's the coolest golf ball ever. If you hit it into the woods, little legs come out of it and it walks back to you. If you hit it into the water, little fins come out and it swims back to shore, and then walks back to you."

His wife says, "Where'd you get it?"

Crane says, "I found it."

|||||||||||||||||||||||

A wagon train's headed to San Francisco and the wagon master calls a meeting.

He says, "Okay, I've got some good news and I've got some bad news. The bad news is there's nothing left to eat except buffalo shit."

Everybody goes, *"Yuckkkk!"*

"And now the good news...there's not enough to go around."

|||||||||||||||||||||||

Barker takes a girl to dinner on their first date.

The waiter comes over and she orders a shrimp and crabmeat cocktail, a Kobe filet, a twice-baked potato, triple vegetables, crème brulée, and then requests a very expensive bottle of wine.

Barker says, "Does your mother feed you like that?"

She says, "No, but my mother's not looking to fuck me, either."

|||||||||||||||||||||||

Beno hands a doctor a note that says, "Dear Doc, I have totally lost the ability to speak. Can you help me?"

The doctor says, "No problem. Take out your penis and put it on that table."

Beno does it, the doctor takes a little rubber mallet and *smashes!* Beno's dick.

Beno goes, *"AAAHHH!"*

The doctor says, "Very good. Come back tomorrow, and we'll start on the Bs."

|||||||||||||||||||||||

Rosenberg's in New York City and he hails a cab. The cab's going down the street when they see a guy on the sidewalk hit a woman over the head. She goes down and the guy starts kicking her. The cabbie *zooms* to the side of the road and jumps out to go help the woman.

Rosenberg rolls down the window and says, "*Stop* it! *Stop* it! Stop the meter!"

|||||||||||||||||||||||

Mayhew's drinking in a bar and every once in a while, the guy next to him tugs on a piece of string that's hanging out of the back of his shirt collar.

After the third time Mayhew says, "Hey, pal, my curiosity's *killing* me...what's with the string?"

The guy says, "You really want to know? Two weeks ago, I had a date with a really cute girl, and when we got into my bed, I couldn't get a hard-on. She played with it, kissed it, sucked it, rubbed oil on it, and...*nothing*. Not a twitch. It made me so fucking mad that now I tie a string to the end of my dick, bring it between my legs, and up the back of my shirt so every time I think of how it let me down, I pull the on the string so my cock can kiss my ass."

|||||||||||||||||||||||

There once was a man from Nantucket,
Whose dick was so long he could suck it...
He said, with a grin,

As he wiped off his chin,
"If my ear were a cunt I would fuck it."   (

|||||||||||||||||||||||

Why don't cannibals eat divorced women?
They're too bitter.

|||||||||||||||||||||||

Stanley says to his brother, "I have to go to England for three weeks, so I have to leave my cat with you. Please take real good care of her."

His brother says, "Relax."

A few days after he gets to England, Stanley calls his brother and says, "How's my cat?"

His brother says, "The cat's dead."

Stanley says, "My *God*. Why'd you have to be so *blunt*? Couldn't you have broken it to me a little more gently? Like, you could have told me the cat was on the roof, and you called the fire department, but just before they got to her, she slipped and fell to the ground, and that you rushed her to the vet but there was nothing he could do to save her..."

His brother says, "Whatever."

Stanley says, "How's Ma?"

His brother says, "*Umm*...Ma's on the roof..."

|||||||||||||||||||||||

Federico turns sixteen and his grandfather gives him a shiny new handgun. Two years later, Federico figures he'll never need the gun and trades it in for a watch.

He walks in the house and his grandfather says, "Federico, where you get-a such a nice-a watch?"

He says, "I got it in trade for the gun you gave me, Pop Pop."

His grandfather says, "What-a, you some kind of *stupido*, Federico? Some-a day soon you gonna find you a woman, you-a gonna marry this-a woman, and then-a one-a day you gonna walk in the house-a and she gonna be in-a bed with-a some-a other man. What you gonna do *then*, Federico? Point to your watch and say, 'Your time, she's-a up-a?'"

|||||||||||||||||||||||

Goodman calls Hartke and says, "Can I stay at your house for a while? My old lady kicked me out after she caught me measuring my dick."

Hartke says, "Sure. So how long is it?"

Goodman says, "Just long enough to reach the back of her sister's throat."

|||||||||||||||||||||||

There's an incredible nuclear blast and everybody in the world dies. Three billion people are waiting in line at the pearly gates when St. Peter comes out and says something to the people out front. Suddenly, up goes the loudest cheer anybody's ever heard.

A guy just out of earshot leans forward and says to the guy in front of him, "What's the cheer for?"

The guy turns to him and says, "St. Peter's not going to count fucking."

|||||||||||||||||||||||

Did you hear about the quadriplegic juggler?
It's so sad. He keeps dropping the quadriplegics.

||||||||||||||||||||||||

Harris goes to visit his friend at work, and he says, "Man, that new secretary of yours is *hot*. She's *gorgeous*."

His friend says, "Yeah, and she's a robot. If you squeeze her left boob, she takes dictation. If you squeeze her *right* boob, she dials the boss. And you can fuck her. Go ahead, take her into the closet."

Harris takes her into the closet, and in a few minutes, his friend hears, "*Yoowwwchh!*"

His friend yells, "Oh, I forgot to tell you...her asshole's a pencil sharpener."

||||||||||||||||||||||||

May those who love us love us...and may those who don't love us, may they one day turn their hearts.

...and if they don't turn their hearts, may they turn their ankles so we'll know them by their limping.

||||||||||||||||||||||||

A Walmart greeter in Cleveland's standing near the entrance with her clipboard when a really, really ugly woman comes in with a five-year-old and a ten-year-old. She's dragging the five-year-old, and bitching at the kids nonstop in a shrill, screeching voice.

The greeter says, "Excuse me, are they twins, ma'am?"

She says, "Of *course* not, you idiot. They're *five years apart*. Why in hell would you think they was twins?"

The greeter says, "I just can't believe anybody would've fucked you twice."

Bales goes into a pet store and says, "My dog ran away. I need another dog."

The pet store owner says, "Come on, it's 2018, you don't want a dog. They're too big, too much hassle, with the food, the walking... you know what you want? This toothless hamster."

Bales says, "Now why would I want a *toothless hamster?*"

The pet store owner says, "Pull down your zipper and I'll show you."

The pet store owner takes the toothless hamster, puts it down by Bales' crotch, the hamster lunges out, and gives Bales the best blow job he's ever had.

Bales buys the hamster. He goes home, walks in the kitchen, and sets the hamster on the floor.

His wife sees it, jumps up on a chair, and screams, "*Ahhh!* What's *that?*"

Bales says, "Never mind what it is. Just teach it how to cook and get the fuck out."

||||||||||||||||||||||||

A cowboy comes bursting into a crowded saloon waving his six-shooter.

He says, "All right, who-all in here's been fuckin' my wife?"

The bartender says, "You're gonna need more ammo."

||||||||||||||||||||||||

Remember, the only way to avoid an alcohol-related accident is to get so fucked up you can't find your car.

||||||||||||||||||||||||

Oglio meets a girl in a bar, they go back to his place, and she gives him an incredible blow job. Then he's lying there, smoking a joint, and she starts stroking his cock. Stroking...and stroking. Five minutes, ten minutes, fifteen minutes...stroking his cock.

Finally he says, "You like that, eh? You want some more?"

She says, "No, I'm just admiring it because I used to have one of my own."

||||||||||||||||||||||||

How's a blind man know when he's done wiping?

The toilet paper stops sticking to his forehead.

||||||||||||||||||||||||

A kid and his girlfriend are sitting on her living room couch, and her parents are in the kitchen watching as he runs to the bathroom every few minutes.

Abe says to his wife, "What's the matter with that boy? I don't like all of this running business. Maybe he's got a disease. Becky, go on, you go ask him what's the matter with him."

The girl's mother meets the kid in the hallway and says, "Why do you keep running to the bathroom?"

The kid says, "Well, your...your daughter's so pretty that every time I look at her, I get an erection. So I keep running to the bathroom to put cold water on it, to keep it down."

She goes back into the kitchen, and Abe says, "Well, what is it? Does he have a disease?"

She says, "*You* should have such a disease."

||||||||||||||||||||||||

A long-haired kid is hitchhiking and gets picked up by a trucker.

After a few miles, he says, "Well, aren't you going to ask me if I'm a *boy* or a *girl*?"

The trucker says, "It don't matter. I'm gonna fuck you anyway."

|||||||||||||||||||||||

An Italian guy goes up to his neighbor and says, "Ey, Tony, you like-a woman with-a big, sloppy tits that droop-a down this-a far?"

Tony says, "No."

He says, "You like-a woman with-a big huge ass like a dump-a truck?"

Tony says, "No."

He says, "You like-a woman with-a big, thick-a moustache and she's a smell like garlic all the time?"

Tony says, "*No*."

He says, "Then why you fuck-a my wife?"

|||||||||||||||||||||||

A little old lady walks into the delicatessen and says to the guy behind the counter, "Have you got assorted nuts?"

He says, "No, lady, I got a matched pair."

|||||||||||||||||||||||

Two Catholic priests are walking down Fifth Avenue when they see Jesus Christ walking towards them.

The first priest turns to the second priest and says, "Try to look busy."

|||||||||||||||||||||||

Three guys are fishing when Fred gets up to get a beer, loses his balance, and falls out of the boat.

Finn says, "What should we do?"

Sniffen says, "You better jump in and help him. He's been under a long time."

So Finn jumps in, and after a while, he comes back up with Fred, and they drag him back into the boat.

Finn says, "What do we do now? It doesn't look like he's breathing."

Sniffen says, "You better give him mouth to mouth."

Finn starts to blow air into Fred's mouth and says, "*Whoa!* I don't remember Fred having such bad breath."

Sniffen says, "Come to think of it, I don't think Fred was wearing a snowmobile suit either."

||||||||||||||||||||||

Two muffins are in an oven, and the first muffin says, "Is it hot in here, or is it me?"

The second muffin says, "Holy fuck! A talking muffin!"

||||||||||||||||||||||

A vet has a very bad day, but when he gets home, his wife is waiting for him with a drink and dinner, and then grabs his hand and leads him to bed.

A few minutes later, the phone rings, and a little old lady says, "I-is this Dr. Cantor?"

He says, "Yeah. Is this an emergency?"

She says, "Y-yes. Y-yes, it is. Th-there's a whole bunch of cats on the roof right outside my window, a-and they're all, they're all fucking, a-and they're making a terrible racket, and I, and I can't get to sleep. Wh-what can I do?"

He says, "Open the window and tell them they're wanted on the phone."

She says, "W-will that stop them?"

The vet says, "It stopped me."

|||||||||||||||||||||||

A shipwrecked crew's in a lifeboat for ten days and they've got nothing left to eat.

The captain says, "I'm going to kill myself and you men can eat my body."

As he lifts a revolver to his ear, one of the men says, "Captain, don't! *Stop!*"

The captain looks over and says, "Why?"

The sailor says, "Please don't shoot yourself in the head. Brains are my favorite dish."

|||||||||||||||||||||||

Legman walks into the kitchen with a sheep under his arm and says, "Darling, this is the pig I fuck when you have a headache."

His wife says, "That's a *sheep*, you idiot."

Legman says, "I wasn't talking to you."

SECTION EIGHT

The Hairy Home Companion

The wife is sexually frustrated so she goes out and buys a pair of crotchless panties. She puts them on under a very short skirt, sits on the sofa in the living room right across from her husband, and keeps crossing and uncrossing her legs.

He looks over and says, "Are you wearing crotchless panties?"

She says, "Yes, I am."

He says, "Thank God. I thought you were sitting on the cat."

|||||||||||||||||||||||

A woman goes up to a guy in a Miami Beach hotel lobby and says, "You must be new, I've never seen you here before."

He says, "To tell you the truth, lady, I just got out of jail. I did thirty years for killing my wife with a hatchet."

She says, "So you're *single*?"

|||||||||||||||||||||||

McCreedy buys his mother-in-law a cemetery plot for a Christmas present. The next year, he doesn't get her a gift.

She says, "Why didn't I get a Christmas gift from you this year?"

He says, "You never used the one I got you last year."

|||||||||||||||||||||||

O'Connell says to his friend, "When I see a woman I want I go right up to her and say, 'I want to fuck you.'"

His friend says, "Wow, you must get smacked a lot."

The first guy says, "Oh, yeah...but I get fucked a lot too."

|||||||||||||||||||||||

A Chinese guy, a Russian guy, an American guy, and a Jewish guy are sitting on a park bench.

A pollster comes up to them and says, "Excuse me, what's your opinion on the meat shortage?"

The Chinese guy says, "What's an opinion?"

The Russian says, "What's meat?"

The American says, "What's a shortage?"

The Jewish guy says, "What's 'excuse me'?"

||||||||||||||||||||||

A wagon train of settlers are deep in Indian territory.

As they're coming to a rise, one of the settlers says, "I don't like the sound of those drums."

An Indian shouts back, "He's not our regular drummer."

||||||||||||||||||||||

Woods says to a girl, "Gimme a blow job."

She says, "Be more romantic."

He says, "Gimme a blow job in the rain."

||||||||||||||||||||||

An old guy calls a repairman.

He says, "Th-there's a leak in the ceiling o-over my kitchen table."

The repairman says, "When did you first notice the leak?"

The old guy says, "L-last night, wh-when it took me two hours to f-finish my soup."

||||||||||||||||||||||

The wife's in the kitchen screaming at her husband, "Get out! *Get the fuck out!*"

As he's walking out the door she yells, "*I hope you die a slow and painful death!*"

He turns and says, "S-so now you want me to *stay*?"

|||||||||||||||||||||||

Did you hear about the guy who's half Greek and half Polish?
His wife got pregnant.

|||||||||||||||||||||||

A dentist walks in with a needle to give Kasten a shot of Novocain.

Kasten says, "No way! No *needles*! I *hate* needles!"

The dentist starts hooking up the nitrous oxide and Kasten says, "No! *No!* I can't do the gas thing either!"

The dentist says, "Can you take a pill?"

Kasten says, "Fine."

The dentist reaches into a drawer, takes out a pill, and says, "Here's a Viagra."

Kasten says, "Wow. I didn't know Viagra worked as a pain killer."

The dentist says, "It doesn't. But it'll going to give you something to hang on to while I'm yanking out your tooth."

|||||||||||||||||||||||

Why do married men gain weight while bachelors don't?
Bachelors go to the refrigerator, see nothing they want, then go to bed...

Married guys go to the bed, see nothing they want, then head to the refrigerator.

IIIIIIIIIIIIIIIIIIII

Sullivan's on a plane and he says to the girl sitting next to him, "I don't mean to intrude, but that's some wedding ring you've got on."

She says, "Thank you. It's a very special gem. It's the tenth largest diamond in the world, the Klopman Diamond. But like many of the great stones in the world, it comes with a curse."

He says, "Oh, really? What's the curse?"

She says, "Mr. Klopman."

IIIIIIIIIIIIIIIIIIIIIIII

Raniolo has an operation on his throat, so the only way he can get nourishment is to be force-fed with a machine through his rectum. After three days of this, he calls for the nurse.

He says, "Nurse, is there another one of these machines in the hospital?"

She says, "Yes, sir."

He says, "Could you roll it in here?"

She says, "Of course, sir, but why?"

He says, "I want you to have lunch with me tomorrow."

IIIIIIIIIIIIIIIIIIIIIIII

An old Jewish guy and a hooker go into an alley and she pulls down his pants and his underpants.

Then she says, "Gimme a hundred bucks."

He hands her a hundred dollars and she runs away.

He says, "So it shouldn't be a *total* loss, I'll take a shit."

IIIIIIIIIIIIIIIIIIIIII

What's the worst thing about anal sex with a horse?
When it's his turn.

IIIIIIIIIIIIIIIIIIIIII

Two old guys are sitting on a park bench and the first guy says, "I'm so old I can't even remember how old I am."

The second guy says, "I can tell you how old you are."

The first guy says, "Oh, yeah?"

The second guy says, "Yeah. Stand up."

He does it.

The second guy says, "Now pull down your pants and your underpants."

He does it.

The second guy says, "Now bend over and stick three fingers as far up your ass as you can."

He does it.

The second guy says, "You're ninety-three."

The first guy says, "How can you tell?"

The second guy says, "You told me yesterday."

IIIIIIIIIIIIIIIIIIIIII

A skeleton walks into a bar.

He says, "Give me a beer and a mop."

IIIIIIIIIIIIIIIIIIIIII

Barmby's in a hotel in a deserted Alaskan town. He comes out of his room and sees another guy in a tuxedo.

He says, "What're you all dressed up for? There's nothing to do in this town."

The other guy says, "We all go to Joe at the end of the hall. If you're nice to his dog, you can fuck Joe in the nose."

Barmby says, "You sick bastard."

A few weeks later, Barmby's really horny and sees the guy in the hall in his tuxedo.

Barmby says, "I want to go with you to see Joe."

The other guy says, "Well, you have to dress up a bit, and be nice to Joe's dog."

Barmby puts on a coat and tie and they go to Joe's room. They walk in, they both pat the dog on the head, Joe smiles, and then they both fuck Joe in the nose.

When they're done, Joe says to Barmby, "Can I ask you two questions?"

Barmby says, "Uh...sure."

Joe says, "Well, first off, did you enjoy it?"

Barmby says, "*Umm*...well, it *was* different. But, you know what? Yeah, in its own weird way, I guess it was pretty good."

Joe says, "And...do you have any diseases?"

Barmby says, "Of *course* not."

Joe goes, "*Snoorrrrttt.*"

|||||||||||||||||||||

Albert Einstein's favorite joke (seriously):
"My dick isn't that big, but I love every foot of it."

|||||||||||||||||||||

A duck walks into the bar and says, "Lemme have a Heineken."
The bartender says, "You can talk."

The duck says, "Of *course* I can talk. I've got a fucking mouth, haven't I?"

The bartender says, "I've never seen you in here before. What do you do?"

The duck says, "I'm the world's best bricklayer. I'm in town to build the new museum."

So the duck stops in every day after work for a beer, and then he leaves.

One day the duck comes in and says, "God *damn* it. Gimme a whole bottle of Tequila."

The bartender says, "What's the matter?"

The duck says, "I finished the museum early and now I'm out of work."

The bartender says, "Well, there's a circus in town. I told the owner all about you, and he says you can get a job with him anytime you want."

The duck says, "A *circus?*"

The bartender says, "Yep."

The duck says, "That's the thing with the tents, right?"

The bartender says, "Yep."

The duck says, "And they hold the tents up with metal poles, right?"

The bartender says, "Yep."

The duck says, "Then why in fuck would they need a *bricklayer?*"

|||||||||||||||||||||||

Hirsch gets a new job so he has to take a physical.

The doctor finishes the exam and says, "*Jesus*, man, you've got the smallest penis I've ever seen. Do you have any difficulties with it being so small?"

Hirsch says, "No. I've got a great wife, two kids, and a normal sex life. I guess the only problem I have is finding it when I have to take a piss."

The doctor says, "You have a problem finding it to urinate? Then how the hell do you have a normal sex life?"

Hirsch says, "Because when we want to *fuck*, there's *two* of us looking for it."

||||||||||||||||||||||

Broderick calls the doctor and says, "Doc, you gotta help me. A mouse ran up inside my wife."

The doctor says, "I'll be right there. In the meantime, wave a piece of cheese between her legs."

The doctor races over, and when he comes in the door, Broderick's waving a herring between his wife's legs.

The doctor says, "What're you *doing*? I said to use a piece of cheese."

Broderick says, "I know you did. But we have to get the cat out first."

||||||||||||||||||||||

What's the difference between toilet paper and toast?
Toast comes up brown on both sides.

||||||||||||||||||||||

Cirella says, "Doc, you gotta cure me of smoking. I'm smoking ten cigars a day."

The doctor says, "That's easy. Before you smoke a cigar, stick it far up your ass."

Two weeks later, Cirella walks back into the doctor's office.

The doctor says, "Did you do what I told you?"

Cirella says, "Yep."

The doctor says, "Did it cure you of smoking?"

Cirella says, "Yep. Now all you have to do is cure me of sticking cigars *farrrr* up my ass."

||||||||||||||||||||||

Galluccio says to his date, "You remind me of my pinky toe."

She says, "Because I'm little and cute?"

He says, "No, because I'm probably going to bang you on my coffee table after I get drunk."

||||||||||||||||||||||

Susie's sixteen, walks into the house at two in the morning, and her mother's waiting for her, mad as hell.

Susie says, "But, Mom, I was with Billy, and I *love* him."

Her mother says, "It's not love, it's infatuation."

Susie says, "But I blew him and then he fucked me in the ass."

Her mother says, "That's infatuation. When he fucks you in the ass and *then* you blow him, *that's* love."

||||||||||||||||||||||

There's a huge seven-alarm bar fire in New York City and trucks are dispatched from all five boroughs. When it's finally under control, one of the fire chiefs walks in and there's two Irish guys standing at the bar.

The chief says, "I can't believe you guys are in here. How'd the fire start?"

One of the Irish guys says, "We've no idea. 'Twas burnin' when we came in."

|||||||||||||||||||||

Stash is out hunting with his brother when his brother says, "Stash, I gotta take a dump."

Stash says, "Go do it in the woods."

A few minutes later his brother yells, "Stash, there's nothin' out here to wipe with. No leaves, no paper, no nothin'."

Stash says, "Use a dollar."

A few minutes later, here comes his brother, his hands and fingers all brown and disgusting.

Stash says, "*Yukk!* What the hell happened to *you*?"

His brother says, "This ain't the worst of it, Stash...I had to throw away the two quarters and the five dimes."

|||||||||||||||||||||

Why can't Stevie Wonder see his friends?
He's married.

|||||||||||||||||||||

Munger's in Kansas City and he needs a job.

He goes into a placement center and he sees a card on the Help Wanted board that says, "Needed: gynecologist's assistant, local."

He says to the girl behind the desk, "Can give me some more information on that gynecologist's assistant job? The card says it's local?"

She says, "Yeah, it's here in Kansas City. The job is to get patients ready for the gynecologist. You help the women out of their clothes and onto the table, wash their genital region...then you lather their genital area with shaving cream, gently shave off all of their pubic hair, and thoroughly rub in warm oil. The annual salary's forty-five thousand dollars, and you'll have to go to Wichita, about a hundred and twenty miles from here."

Munger says, "*Hey!* I thought you just said the job was *local*, that it was here in Kansas City?"

She says, "It is. But Wichita's where the end of the line is."

||||||||||||||||||||||||

Why did the guy marry the Siamese twin?
So he could fuck his wife and have a girlfriend on the side.

||||||||||||||||||||||||

Washburn says to his doctor, "Doc, you gotta help me. Every morning I wake up and fuck my wife. I carpool with the neighbor's wife, and on the way to work she gives me a blow job. Whenever I go into the copy room, I bang one of the office girls up on the machine. At lunch, I take my secretary to a hotel and fuck her in her ass, because that's the way she likes it. During the afternoon coffee break, I fuck the boss's wife. Then I go home and the maid either sucks my cock or bends over so I can give it to her doggie style. And then at night, I fuck my wife again."

The doctor says, "So what's your problem?"

He says, "It hurts when I jerk off."

||||||||||||||||||||||||

Two old ladies are sitting at the slot machines at the Borgata in Atlantic City.

The first one says, "D-did you come on the bus?"

The second one says, "Yeah, b-but I made it look like an asthma attack."

|||||||||||||||||||||||

A little kid sits on his grandfather's lap and says, "Pop Pop, would you make a noise like a frog?"

The old guy says, "Wh-why?"

The kid says, "Because Mom says when Grandpa croaks we're all going to Disney World."

|||||||||||||||||||||||

Schmidlap's in Europe and he gets a phone call.

The voice says, "Mr. Schmidlap, your mother-in-law passed away. Should we cremate her or bury her?"

He says, "Don't take any chances. Do both."

|||||||||||||||||||||||

What do you get when you cross an Italian dictator with a black guy?

Moosecockolini.

|||||||||||||||||||||||

A guy walks into a bar. There's a beautiful blonde bar maid and behind her's a sign that says, "Cheese Sandwich, five dollars. Chicken Sandwich, seven dollars. Hand Job, fifty dollars."

He says, "You the one who gives the hand jobs?"

She says, "Yep."

He says, "Wash your hands and make me a cheese sandwich."

|||||||||||||||||||||||

Nelson walks in really late and really drunk and his wife's standing there holding a broom.

He says, "A-are you still cleaning o-or are you going for a ride?"

||||||||||||||||||||||

Cumia says to his wife, "What would you do if I won the lottery?"

She says, "I'd take half and leave."

He says, "Well, I won twelve bucks. Here's six. Now get the fuck out."

||||||||||||||||||||||

A professor's teaching a night school class on Sex Ed.

He says, "Let's take a simple survey. How many of you have sex once a day?"

A bunch of people raise their hands.

He says, "How many of you have sex once a week?"

A lot of people raise their hands.

He says, "How many of you have sex once a month?"

A bunch of people raise their hands.

He says, "And how many of you have sex once a year?"

A guy in the back starts jumping up and down, yelling, "Me! *Me!* Right here! *Me!*"

The professor says, "If you only have sex once a year, why are you so excited?"

The guy says, "Because *tonight's the night! Tonight's the night!*"

SECTION NINE

Coney Island Whitefish

Marci goes up to the drugstore counter and says, "I'd like a box of condoms."

The pharmacist says, "Don't want to have any kids, eh?"

Marci says, "No, my boyfriend doesn't want to get any shit on his cock."

|||||||||||||||||||||||

Mrs. Ward takes her clothes to a Chinese laundry and when it comes back she sees there are still stains in her panties.

The next week she puts in a note, "Please use more soap on panties."

When she gets them back there's a note, "Please use more paper on ass."

|||||||||||||||||||||||

A baby polar bear goes up to his mother and says, "Mom, am I pure polar bear?"

His mother says, "Of course you're pure polar bear. I'm a polar bear and your father's a polar bear."

The cub says, "But am I a *hundred percent* pure polar bear?"

She says, "Go ask your old man."

The baby polar bear goes up to his father and says, "Pop, am I pure polar bear? I mean, a *hundred percent* pure polar bear?"

His father says, "Of *course* you're a hundred percent pure polar bear. I'm a polar bear, your mother's a polar bear, both my parents were polar bears, both of your mother's parents were polar bears, all of our grandparents both sides were polar bears...yes, you're a hundred percent pure polar bear. Why do you ask?"

The cub says, "Because I'm fucking *freezing!*"

|||||||||||||||||||||||

A cowboy's riding along and sees an Indian up on a hill with his pants down. The Indian's got a huge hard-on, and he keeps looking up at the sun and then down at the ground.

The cowboy rides up and says, "What in tarnation are you doing?"

The Indian says, "Me tell-um time with cock and sun. It three-thirty."

The cowboy looks at his watch and it's three-thirty.

The cowboy says, "Now how the heck did you go and do that?"

The Indian says, "Me no tell. Heap big Indian secret."

A few days later the cowboy's riding along and sees the same Indian on the same hill, only this time the Indian's got his pants down and he's jerking wildly on his cock.

The cowboy yells up, "What in tarnation are you doing *now*?"

The Indian says, "Wind-um watch."

|||||||||||||||||||||||||

When did Pinocchio realize he was made of wood?
The day his hand caught fire.

|||||||||||||||||||||||||

Two girls are driving along in the country when the girl driving says, "I gotta whiz."

Her friend says, "Me too. Pull over."

They pull off the road, jump over the fence, and it's a graveyard. The first girl goes behind a headstone, there's nothing to wipe with, she wipes with her panties and tosses them. The second girl goes behind a headstone, there's nothing to wipe with, but she's next to freshly dug grave, so she takes a ribbon from a wreath and wipes with that. The next day the two husbands are talking on the phone.

The first husband says, "We better keep an eye on our wives. Yesterday my wife came home with no panties."

The second husband says, "That's nothing. My wife came home with a card stuck to her ass that said, 'We're all really gonna miss you.'"

||||||||||||||||||||||

What's the difference between a regular inflatable doll and a senior citizen's inflatable doll?
The senior citizen's inflatable doll you only blow up halfway.

||||||||||||||||||||||

Dixon drives into a Wyoming town and sees a cowboy chasing a coyote down Main Street. The cowboy catches one of its legs, yanks down his pants, grabs the coyote's other leg, and fucks it like he's pushing a wheelbarrow. After he sees that, Dixon needs a drink, so he goes into a saloon and there's an old guy sitting at a table jerking off.

The sheriff walks into the saloon and Dixon says, "Jesus Christ, what kind of town *is* this? First I see a guy fucking a coyote on Main Street, and now this old geezer's sitting in the bar jacking off."

The sheriff says, "Now you don't expect an old man to be able to catch a coyote, do you?"

||||||||||||||||||||||

How do you get a gay guy to fuck a woman?
Shit in her cunt.

||||||||||||||||||||||

A young couple has sex, and when they're finished, she looks in the box of condoms, and there's only six left out of the twelve.

She says, "What happened to the other condoms?"

He says, "I, uh...I made balloon animals out of them for my niece and nephew."

That night she's out to dinner with a guy friend and tells him what happened, and she says, "Have you ever done that?"

He says, "Of course. All the time."

She says, "*Really?* You make balloon animals out of condoms?"

He says, "Oh, no. I thought you were asking me if I've ever lied to my girlfriend."

||||||||||||||||||||||

Haggerty says to his wife, "Have you been sucking off the dog?"

She says, "Why do you ask?"

He says, "Because every time you yawn he gets a hard-on."

||||||||||||||||||||||

Clarke walks into a department store and a really cute salesgirl says, "What would you like?"

He says, "I'd like to suck on your pussy until your head caves in; what I *need* is a pair of socks."

||||||||||||||||||||||

Two psychiatrists are walking along and there's a guy coming the other way. Just as the guy's passing them, he turns and spits right in the first psychiatrist's face. And the psychiatrist keeps walking.

The second psychiatrist says, "Aren't you going to do something about that?"

The first psychiatrist says, "Why should I? It's *his* problem."

|||||||||||||||||||||

Favale walks into a bar, sits down next to a girl, and as they're drinking, he keeps looking at his watch.

Finally she says, "Are you meeting somebody here? Is she late?"

Favale says, "No. I've got this new state-of-the-art watch, and I'm thinking about testing it."

The girl says, "A state-of-the-art watch? What does it do?"

Favale says, "It uses alpha waves to telepathically talk to me."

She says, "What's it telling you now?"

Favale says, "*Hmm*...it says you're not wearing panties."

She says, "Well, it's wrong, because I do have panties on."

Favale says, "*Hmm*...must be an hour fast."

|||||||||||||||||||||

Jackman's fingering his big fat girlfriend.

She says, "Would you mind taking off your ring? It's scratching me."

Jackman says, "That's not my ring. It's my *wristwatch*."

|||||||||||||||||||||

How can you tell it's a debutante giving you a hand job?
She crooks her pinkie.

|||||||||||||||||||||

A seventy-five-year-old guy's in the same nursing home as his ninety-seven-year-old mother; it's her birthday and he's got no money for a gift.

Being a thoughtful son, he goes into her room and says, "Mom,

I got no present for you, so to celebrate your birthday, why don't we just fuck?"

They get naked, climb on the bed, and get to it. After a few minutes of huffing and puffing, the old girl starts shitting like mad all over the bed.

He says, "Jesus *Christ*, Ma, what's going on?"

She says, "W-well, I'm way too old t-to have an orgasm, a-and I wanted to do something to show you h-how much I was enjoying myself."

|||||||||||||||||||||||

A married couple goes to the same Chinese restaurant every Sunday for thirty years.

Every time they walk in the owner says, "*Herro!* You my *favorite* couple. You made for each other. Rast so rong. You *meant* to *be!*"

One Sunday the guy walks in alone.

The Chinese guy says, "Wha hoppen?"

The guy says, "We got a divorce."

The Chinese guy says, "Oh, you much-a betta off now."

|||||||||||||||||||||||

A kid says to his father, "Pop, I wanna be a musician when I grow up."

His father says, "You can't do both, son."

|||||||||||||||||||||||

Ireland's never been known for its swimming, but one day the Irish Parliament decides they're going to assemble a swim team for the next Olympics.

They put an ad in the paper, "Swimmers Wanted For The Irish Swim Team."

One day there's a knock on the door at the fieldhouse, the swim team captain opens it, and there's a guy with no legs.

The captain says, "Can I help you, lad?"

The guy says, "I'm here to try out for the swim team."

The captain says, "But you've no legs."

The legless guy says, "But I can swim, mate. Toss me in the pool."

The captain tosses him in the pool and the legless guy zooms from one end of the pool to the other.

The captain says, "You're in."

The next day there's a knock on the door, the captain opens it, and there's a guy with no arms and no legs.

The captain says, "What is it you want, son?"

The guy says, "I'm here to try out for the swim team."

The captain says, "But you've no arms nor legs."

The armless legless guy says, "Never mind that. Toss me in the pool."

The swim captain tosses him in the pool and the guy with no arms and no legs quickly wiggles his way from one end of the pool to the other.

The swim captain says, "I can't believe it. We can use you."

The next day there's a knock on the door, the captain opens it, and there's a head. No body, just a head.

The swim captain says, "Can I help you?"

The head says, "I'm here to try out for the swim team."

The swim captain says, "But...you're but a *head*. Just a bloody head."

The head says, "Yes, that's true...but I can swim like a fish. Please toss me in the pool."

The captain tosses the head in the pool and the head sinks like a stone.

The captain jumps in, brings the head up, and puts it on a chair.

The head coughs up some water, and then says, "Hell of a time to get a cramp, eh?"

||||||||||||||||||||||

How is broccoli like anal sex?

If it was forced on you as a kid, you probably won't enjoy it as an adult.

||||||||||||||||||||||

A little old lady calls a plumber. He doesn't show, so she goes shopping. Just after she leaves, the plumber knocks on her door.

Inside, her parrot says, *"Who is it?"*

The plumber says, "It's the plumber, lady."

A few seconds later the parrot says, *"Who is it?"*

The plumber says, "It's the *plumber*, lady."

A few seconds later, the parrot says, *"Who is it?"*

The plumber says, "It's the *plumber*! I *told* you, it's the...*arghh!*"

He has a heart attack and collapses dead on the steps.

A while later the lady comes up her walk and says, "I-I wonder who this is o-on my steps..."

The parrot says, *"It's the plumber."*

||||||||||||||||||||||

How's a puppy like a nearsighted gynecologist?

They've both got a wet nose.

||||||||||||||||||||||

Donald and Melania Trump are riding in a limo in New York City and have the driver stop when they see a sign, "Live Sex Show."

They go inside, sit in the front row, and on a small stage a man and a woman are lying naked on separate couches. The woman's tossing donuts and ringing them on his hard-on, and he's tossing cherries into her twat.

On the way home, Trump looks over and says, "That looked like fun, Melania. Why don't we give it a try?"

She says, "All right. Have the driver stop at a grocery store and we'll pick up a roll of Lifesavers and a dozen grapefruit."

|||||||||||||||||||||||||

What's Derek Jeter call it when he gets a blow job from Siamese twins?

A doubleheader.

|||||||||||||||||||||||||

Sweeney's wife disappears, he doesn't hear from her for two weeks, and then he gets a phone call from a detective.

The detective says, "Well, my friend, I've got good news and bad news. The bad news is your wife is dead. We found her at the bottom of the East River. The good news is there was a huge, perfect black pearl in her vagina. What would you like us to do?"

Sweeney says, "Put the black pearl in a Federal Express envelope, send it to me immediately, and then re-set the trap."

SECTION TEN

Giggle Mortis

Saks's wife passes away. At the wake, his best friend Lewis leaves the viewing to take a leak and spots Saks in the broom closet getting sucked off by the funeral director's wife.

Lewis says, "*Saks!* What in the name of all that's decent are you *doing?*"

Saks says, "In *my* grief, I should know what I'm doing?"

|||||||||||||||||||||||

Two guys are drinking and the first guy says, "When I'm lying there in my casket, I'd like to hear them say that I was a brilliant guy, a nice guy, and a good family man."

The second guy says, "I'd like to hear them say, 'I think I saw him *move.*'"

|||||||||||||||||||||||

Ollie says to Magda, "Honey, it's Tuesday, and we're getting married on Saturday. Can we get undressed and have a bit of fun?"

She says, "No, Ollie, you'll have to wait until Saturday."

He says, "Well, how about letting me have just a little sniff, then?"

She figures that's harmless, so she pulls up her dress and pulls down her panties so Ollie can have a whiff. He puts his face right up to her very hairy crotch and takes a *deeeep* breath.

He pushes her away, looks up, and says, "Magda, sweet, I'm not sure this thing is gonna *keep* 'til Saturday."

|||||||||||||||||||||||

Downing's kneeling at his wife's coffin and a friend kneels down next to him.

His friend says, "Hey, I know it's tough. But in a few weeks, you'll start to feel better, and start to date, and eventually meet another nice woman."

Downing says, "I know. But what am I gonna do *tonight*?"

||||||||||||||||||||||||

Melillo's on a business trip in Japan. His Japanese hosts take him out, get him drunk, and send him upstairs with a hooker.

As he's fucking her she starts screaming, "Nashagai ana! *Nashagai ana!*"

He's thinking, "Yeah, baby, take it all...take it all..."

He keeps pumping and she keeps screaming, "Nashagai ana! *Nashagai ana!*"

The next day the Melillo's playing golf with one of the Japanese businessmen. He tees off and slices the ball *wayyy* off to the right.

The Japanese guy says, "Ahh...nashagai ana."

Melillo says, "What's that mean?"

The Japanese guy says, "Wrong hole."

||||||||||||||||||||||||

Where do midgets go after grade school?
Not So High.

||||||||||||||||||||||||

Hamell's wife's been in a coma for ten years. For the entire time, she's never spoken or moved at all. Then one day a nurse is giving her a sponge bath and as the sponge rubs across Hamell's wife's twat, she moans. The nurse gets the doctor, the doctor tries it, and she moans again.

The doctor calls Hamell and says, "Mr. Hamell, you must get to the hospital immediately."

When Hamell gets there, the doctor says, "We have a breakthrough. I think a little oral sex might snap your wife out of it. Go into her room and we'll monitor her from out here in the hall."

Hamell goes into his wife's room, and the doctor and the nurse watch her heart monitor go, "*bleep...bleep...*" ...and then die out. She completely flatlines. They run into the room and see Hamell pulling up his pants.

The doctor says, "What happened?"

Hamell says, "I think she choked to death."

||||||||||||||||||||||

What do you call it when you have anal sex with your father's sister?

Up the ante.

||||||||||||||||||||||

A woman's in bed fucking her husband's best friend when the phone rings.

She answers it and says, "*Hello?* Oh, hi. So glad you called. *Really?* That's great. I'm so happy for you, it sounds like fun. *Great!* Thanks. Okay, bye."

The guy says, "Who was that?"

She says, "That was my husband telling me what a great time you and he are having on your fishing trip."

||||||||||||||||||||||

Shapiro's packing for a business trip and his three-year-old daughter's having a great time playing on the bed.

She says, "Daddy, look!" and sticks out two of her fingers.

He leans over, sticks her tiny fingers in his mouth, and says,

"Daddy's gonna eat your fingers," pretends to eat them, and then goes back to packing.

When he looks up again his daughter's standing on the bed staring at her fingers looking very disappointed.

He says, "What's the matter, honey?"

She says, "What happened to my booger?"

||||||||||||||||||||||

Charlie gets a job as a boil sucker, sucking boils off of people. His first appointment, he knocks on the door and a big fat lady answers. They go into her kitchen, she pulls up her dress, and she's got a huge boil just under the left cheek of her ass.

Charlie puts his mouth around the boil, and just as he starts sucking as hard as he can, she lets out a *huge* fart...*llbbtt!*

Charlie says, "You know, lady, it's people like you that make my job disgusting."

||||||||||||||||||||||

What's the best way to keep kitty litter fresh?
Kill your cat.

||||||||||||||||||||||

Dunn and Walsh are about to start a round of golf when Dunn says, "I wish I was a lesbian."

Walsh says, "Why's that?"

Dunn says, "So I could eat pussy and use the red tees."

||||||||||||||||||||||

A lady has a baby and it's just a head. Nothing but a head. Just a doggone head. That's all it is, a head. What's she gonna do? She puts it at the top of the stairs on a table facing out the window.

Eighteen years the head's there on the table facing out the window. Finally, one day the phone rings, she answers it, and it's the hospital.

A doctor tells her, "Mrs. Johnson, there's been a terrible accident. Someone was decapitated. But we saved the body, and we can put your head...well, not *your* head, but your *head's* head...the head you have at home, we can put it on top of the body and you can have a regular son after all these years."

Needless to say, the lady is tickled pink.

She goes running up the stairs and says, "Bobby! *Bobby!* I've got the most wonderful surprise for you!"

He says, "I hope it's not another fuckin' hat."

|||||||||||||||||||||

An old guy walks into the living room and stands behind the chair where his wife's sitting watching television.

He says, "Hey, you miserable old twat, I stopped and got batteries for your hearing aid."

She says, "I walked down and got them this morning."

|||||||||||||||||||||

A ham sandwich walks into a bar.

The bartender says, "I'm sorry, we don't serve food."

|||||||||||||||||||||

A couple wakes up one morning and the guy says to his wife, "What a party I went to last night, right here in the neighborhood.

Good food, good people, good conversation...and the best thing of all, they had a golden toilet."

She says, "You're crazy. There's no such thing as a golden toilet."

He says, "I'm telling you they had a golden toilet. Right here in the neighborhood. Come on, let's go check it out."

He finds his way to the house where the party was, knocks on the door, and a lady answers.

He says, "Excuse me, lady, would you please show my wife the golden toilet?"

She turns and yells, "Hey, *Ernie!* Here's the guy who wrecked your tuba!"

||||||||||||||||||||||

A cannibal and his son are walking in the jungle when a beautiful girl runs in front of them.

The son says, "Hey, Pop! Let's take her home and eat her."

His father says, "No, let's take her home and eat your *mother.*"

||||||||||||||||||||||

Three gay guys are at a wake talking about their deceased pal.

The first guy says, "After he's cremated, I'd like to toss his ashes off a boat, because we had *such* fun sailing."

The second guy says, "After he's cremated, I'd like to spread his ashes on my garden, because he so loved when I brought him flowers."

The third guy says, "After he's cremated, I'd like to sprinkle his ashes on some hot chili, so he can tear my asshole apart one last time."

||||||||||||||||||||||

An escaped convict breaks into a young couple's house and ties them up.

The husband turns to his wife and says, "Honey, this guy hasn't had any sex for years. Please, do anything he says...our lives depend on it."

She says, "I'm glad you feel that way, because I just heard him mumble to himself that you have a really nice ass."

||||||||||||||||||||||||

Luigi gets in bed, kisses his wife, and goes to sleep. He wakes up in the middle of the night and there's a guy in a long white robe at the foot of his bed.

Luigi says, "What'ya doin' in Luigi's a-bedroom?"

The guy says, "This isn't your bedroom, Luigi. I'm St. Peter and this is Heaven."

Luigi says, "Oh, no, I'm-a not dead yet. You send-a me back to Earth, right-a now."

St. Peter says, "Well, the best I can do is to send you back as a hen."

Luigi says, "That's okay, I'm just not-a dead..."

Poof! Luigi's in a barnyard.

He says, "That's-a not so bad. Got-a nice feathers. Not-s too crazy about the feet-a."

A rooster comes up to Luigi and says, "You must be the new hen."

Luigi says, "Yeah, I'm-a Luigi. I...uhh! *uhh!* My sto-machh, she's-a hurt!"

The rooster says, "You're just ovulating. Lay an egg."

Luigi goes, "Unh! *Unh!* Ey, not-a bad, Luigi lay-a egg. I...uhh! *uhh!* My sto-*machh!*"

The rooster says, "Just lay another egg."

Luigi goes, "*Unh!*"

His wife shakes him and says, "Luigi! *Wake up!* You shit the bed!"

IIIIIIIIIIIIIIIIIIIIIII

An IRS agent calls the synagogue and says, "Rabbi, do you have a parishioner named Ira Mandelbaum?"

The rabbi says, "Yes, we do."

The agent says, "Did he donate twenty-five thousand dollars to the synagogue building fund?"

The rabbi says, "He *will*."

IIIIIIIIIIIIIIIIIIIIIII

A lady comes home after visiting her relatives for two weeks and finds that her husband, who was too lazy to go to the supermarket, ate all the dog food in the house.

She calls the doctor and says, "Doc, you have to do something. My husband ate a half a case of dog food."

The doctor says, "Relax, ma'am, it can't hurt him. There's nothing to worry about."

The next day, the doctor answers his phone, and it's the lady again.

She says, "Nothing to worry about, huh, doc? Well, I hope you're satisfied. My husband's *dead*."

The doctor says, "*Dead?* From eating *dog food?* I can't understand it. What happened?"

She says, "He was lying in the driveway licking himself and I backed the car over him."

IIIIIIIIIIIIIIIIIIIIIII

An old couple's sitting in the living room.

The wife turns to her husband and says, "Let's go upstairs and *fuck*."

He says, "I-I don't know if I can do *both*."

112

|||||||||||||||||||||||

It's a very cold winter's night so three homeless guys huddle up close to stay warm.

When they wake up in the morning, the guy on the left says, "I had a dream somebody was pulling on my dick."

The guy on the right says, "I had a dream somebody was pulling on *my* dick."

The guy in the middle says, "I-I had a dream I went *skiing*."

|||||||||||||||||||||||

Ingegno walks into a bar all upset.

The bartender says, "What's the matter?"

Ingegno says, "Ahh, I had a fight with my wife and she told me she wasn't going to talk to me for a month."

The bartender says, "That sucks."

Ingegno says, "You're not kidding. The month is up today."

|||||||||||||||||||||||

How do you sell a duck to a deaf person?

"YOU WANT TO BUY A DUCK?"

|||||||||||||||||||||||

Two guys are in a doctor's waiting room.

The first guy says, "Why're you here?"

The second guy says, "Endoscopy. He's going down my throat with a camera. Why're *you* here?"

The first guy says, "Camera up the ass."

The second guy says, "Oh, a colonoscopy?"

The first guy says, "No, my wife caught me taking pictures of the neighbor girl sunbathing naked."

||||||||||||||||||||

A trucker goes into a whorehouse, hands the madam five hundred dollars, and says, "I want your ugliest woman and a bologna sandwich."

The madam says, "For that kind of money, you could have one of my finest girls and surf and turf."

The trucker says, "I ain't *horny*—I'm *homesick*."

||||||||||||||||||||

Two eagles are flying side by side when a jet *zooms!* past them.

The first eagle says, "Man, did you see how *fast* that thing was going?"

The second eagle says, "You'd be going that fast too if *your* asshole was on fire."

||||||||||||||||||||

The just-married Blooms are in Las Vegas for their honeymoon and they go to see a show starring "The Amazing Watson."

The Amazing Watson walks out on stage, puts three walnuts on a table, takes out his hard-on, and *smashes!* the walnuts.

Years later, the Blooms are in Las Vegas celebrating their fiftieth anniversary and they see a sign in front of the same club that says, "Tonight! The Amazing Watson!"

And they go in to see the show, because it helps the joke.

The Amazing Watson walks out on stage, puts three coconuts on a table, takes out his hard-on, and *smashes!* the coconuts.

After the show, they go backstage, and Mrs. Bloom says, "Mr.

Watson, fifty years ago you smashed walnuts. Why'd you switch to coconuts?"

Watson says, "Well, you see, at my age, the eyesight starts to go..."

|||||||||||||||||||||||||

The papa shark and the baby shark are gliding up to a bunch of people frolicking in the ocean when the papa shark says, "First we'll swim around them a few times with just the tip of our fins showing."

After they do it, the papa shark says, "Now we'll swim around them a few times with our fins sticking all the way out of the water."

After they do that, the papa shark says, "Now we'll eat them."

After they've eaten everybody, the baby shark says, "Pop, why didn't we just eat them right away? What was with all the swimming around them nonsense?"

The papa shark says, "They're much tastier when there's no shit inside."

|||||||||||||||||||||||||

How do you know when your girlfriend's getting fat?
You start fucking your wife.

|||||||||||||||||||||||||

A guy *smashes!* into the car in front of him. The other driver gets out and it's a dwarf.

The dwarf walks over, looks at the damage, comes to the guy's window and says, "I'm not happy."

The other driver says, "Well, then, which one are you?"

|||||||||||||||||||||||||

Grossman goes up to a girl in a bar and says, "Would you like to come home with me?"

She says, "And why should I?"

He says, "Because I'm a nice guy with a good job."

She says, "What do you do?"

He says, "I'm a dentist."

She says, "Okay, what the hell?" She goes home with him and they get it on.

When they get done, she says, "Hey, you must be a great dentist."

He says, "Why do you say that?"

She says, "I didn't feel a thing."

|||||||||||||||||||||||||

Have you heard about those new super-sensitive condoms?
After you fuck her, they *stay and talk to her.*

SECTION ELEVEN

St. John in the Behind

Dirty Johnny's in the confessional and says, "Father, I can't stop jerking off. All I do is jerk off. Today I already jerked off twenty-two times."

The priest says, "I think you need more than to just confess, son. Go sit in one of the front pews and wait for me."

Mrs. Pascucci knocks on the confessional door and says, "Father, I'm here to make a confession, but I also brought you a homemade cheesecake."

He says, "Thank you so much. Please put it on the pew next to John and come in."

She puts the cheesecake on the pew next to Johnny, goes in, makes her confession, and leaves. The priest comes out, walks over to Johnny, and there's an empty plate on the pew next to him.

The priest says, "Where's the cheesecake?"

Johnny says, "I ate it."

The priest says, "You *ate* it? Why?"

Johnny says, "I had nothing else to do, so I ate it."

The priest says, "Why didn't you jerk off?"

||||||||||||||||||||||

How is eggs Benedict like a blow job?
You can't get either of them at home.

||||||||||||||||||||||

Dowd goes to the doctor for a thorough examination before the start of the hockey season. He strips naked and the doctor checks him over from head to toe. The last thing the doctor does is put a tongue depressor in Dowd's mouth and look down his throat.

The doctor says, "Well, Mr. Dowd, it appears you've got flat feet."

Dowd says, "Doc, you want to do me a favor? Look up my ass and tell me if my hat's on straight?"

||||||||||||||||||||||

Mullin walks into a show business agent's office carrying a little black bag.

The agent says, "Well, let's see your act."

Mullin reaches into the black bag and takes out a hammer and a few walnuts. He puts the walnuts on his head and *smashes!* them with the hammer.

He says to the agent, "Well, what do you think?"

The agent says, "That's your act?"

Mullin says, "Yep."

The agent says, "What else have you got in the black bag?"

Mullin says, "Aspirin."

||||||||||||||||||||||

Nastri walks into a bar, holds out his hand, and says to the bartender, "Look what I almost stepped in."

||||||||||||||||||||||

A new monk arrives to join the others copying ancient records and notices they're copying by hand books that had already been copied by hand.

He says, "Forgive me, but copying other copies by hand allows many chances for error. How do we know we aren't copying somebody else's *mistakes?*"

The head monk says, "That's a good point, my son. I will take one of these new copies down to my vault and study it against the original document."

The old monk goes into the vault to study. The day passes, it's getting late in the evening, and the other monks start to get worried about him, so one of them goes looking for him. As he's walking through the catacombs, he hears sobbing.

He says, "Holy Father?"

The sobbing gets louder as he gets near. Finally, he finds the old priest sitting at a table with both the new copy and the original ancient book in front of him.

He says, "Father, what's wrong?"

The old monk says, "The word is *celebrate*."

|||||||||||||||||||||||

Two flies land on a piece of shit. The first fly lifts his leg and—*lbbtt*—blasts a huge fart.

The second fly says, "*Jesus*, man, I'm trying to *eat*."

|||||||||||||||||||||||

Drezen calls Artsis and says, "Hey, man, I need to come over. I want to jerk off but my computer's down."

Artsis says, "Jesus Christ, Drezen, your girlfriend lives five minutes away. If you're that desperate, why not just go to her house?"

Drezen says, "She hasn't got internet."

|||||||||||||||||||||||

Falato's in a bar.

He taps the guy next to him on the shoulder and says, "You know what you do if an epileptic's having a fit in the bathtub? You throw in your laundry."

The guy says, "Listen, pal, I don't think that's funny. My brother was epileptic and he died in the bathtub during a fit."

Falato says, "Wow, I'm sorry. Did he drown?"
The guy says, "No, he choked on a sock."

||||||||||||||||||||||||

A woman calls Dirty Johnny's mother and says, "I caught your son playing doctors and nurses with my eight-year-old daughter."
Johnny's mother says, "Well, of course they're curious about sex at that age."
The girl's mother says, "*Curious about sex?* He took her fucking *appendix* out."

||||||||||||||||||||||||

Why do men take showers?
Pissing in the bathtub is disgusting.

||||||||||||||||||||||||

The general's about to go into battle and he can't decide which uniform to wear.
One of his aides says, "Well, General, whenever *Napoleon* was about to go into battle, he'd put on a *red* uniform. That way, if he was wounded, his men wouldn't be able to tell, and they wouldn't panic."
The general says, "Very good, Stukowski. Get me my brown uniform."

||||||||||||||||||||||||

What's the difference between a dame and a doughnut?
You can't eat the hole in the doughnut.

|||||||||||||||||||||||

A drunk stumbles out of a bar and there's a nun walking down the sidewalk. He goes up and *punches!* her in the face. Before she can say anything, he *punches!* her in the stomach. She doubles over, he *smacks!* her on the back of the head and she goes down. He *kicks!* her a few times and then he picks her up and *smashes!* her up against a wall.

He says, "Y-you're not too fucking tough *tonight*, a-are you, Batman?"

|||||||||||||||||||||||

Sirota's on the road and goes up to a girl in a bar.

He says, "You want a drink?"

She says, "Sure. I'm a good sport."

They drink the drink and he says, "Want to go back to my hotel?"

She says, "Sure. I'm a good sport."

They get to his hotel room and he says, "You want to get naked?"

She says, "Sure. I'm a good sport."

They get it on and she leaves.

A few months later she calls Sirota at his office and says, "I'm pregnant. I think I'm going to kill myself."

He says, "Geez...you *are* a good sport."

|||||||||||||||||||||||

The synagogue has a raffle. Levy wins third prize and he gets a television. Einhorn wins second prize and he gets an apple pie.

Einhorn says, "Levy, you win *third* prize, and you get a *television*, and I win *second* prize, and I get an *apple pie*? This is *bullshit*."

Levy says, "That pie was baked by the rabbi's wife."

Einhorn says, "*Fuck* the rabbi's wife."

Levy says, "That's *first* prize."

|||||||||||||||||||||||||

How do you know when a woman's too old to fuck?

She breaks her hip jerking you off.

|||||||||||||||||||||||||

Freismuth's rich and one day he decides he wants to cross the Sahara Desert by caravan. He goes to Cairo, buys a small herd of camels, hires Arabs to ride the camels and lead him, gets the supplies they'll need, gives the camels as long a drink of water as they'll take, and they set off, headed west. Sixty miles into the journey, the camels start to drop dead of dehydration one by one. When he's down to his last four camels, Freismuth can't believe his eyes when a caravan of the oldest and most flea-bitten camels he's ever seen come up on them and are about to pass them.

He runs over to the guy at the front of the other caravan and says, "My camels are dropping from dehydration and these old nags of yours look healthy as they can be. What's the story?"

The other guy says, "Well, before you set out to cross the Sahara, you have to give the camels a really long drink of water."

Freismuth says, "I *did*, I *did*."

The other guy says, "And did you brick 'em?"

Freismuth says, "*Brick 'em?* I have no idea what that means."

The other guy says, "Oh, man, to cross the Sahara, you gotta brick 'em. When you're ready to set out, you line the camels up so they'll drink one after the other. You get a brick in each hand and stand behind each camel as he's taking his drink. When you hear the *sluurrrppp* of his drink slowing down and about to come to an end, you smack the bricks together on his balls. He'll go *SLLUURRPPP!*

and suck in enough water to cross the Sahara and probably cross back."

Freismuth says, "But...but doesn't that *hurt*?"

The other guy says, "Well, hell yeah. You gotta be careful not to catch your fingers between the bricks."

|||||||||||||||||||||||||

Why do most women live longer than men?
Because most women aren't married to women.

|||||||||||||||||||||||||

It's 1973, Elvis is big and fat, and he's in the middle of a concert at the *Las Vegas International Hotel.*

He's singing, "Love me tender..."

He stops, looks down at a pretty girl, and says, "What's your name, honey?"

"Karen."

"Where're you from?"

"Providence."

"I played Providence."

"I know, Elvis. I saw you."

He keeps singing, "Love me true..."

He stops and looks down at another pretty girl and says, "What's your name, honey?"

"Rose Ann."

"Where're you from?"

"Del Ray Beach."

"I played Del Ray Beach."

"I know, Elvis. I saw you."

He keeps singing, "Love me tender..."

He stops and looks down at another pretty girl and says, "What's your name, honey?"

"Bernadette."

He says, "Can I ask you a question, honey?"

She says, "Sure, Elvis."

He says, "Are you gonna finish that potato?"

||||||||||||||||||||

Berger's tossing peanuts into the air and catching them in his mouth when his wife asks him a question. As he turns to answer, the peanut falls into his ear. He tries to dig it out, but that only pushes it in deeper, so they decide to go to the hospital. As they're about to leave, their daughter comes in with her date.

After they explain, the daughter's date says, "I can get the peanut out."

He shoves two fingers into Berger's nose, and says, "Blow hard."

Berger *blows!* and the peanut flies out of his ear.

Berger's wife turns to him and says, "Isn't he smart? I wonder what he plans to be."

Berger says, "From the smell of his fingers, it better be our son-in-law."

||||||||||||||||||||

What's white and goes up?

A retarded snowflake.

||||||||||||||||||||

Mrs. Silverman says to her husband, "Hermie, you want some breakfast? Bacon and eggs, some toast? Maybe a half a grapefruit, a cup of coffee?"

125

He says, "No, it's the *Viagra*, it's really taken the edge off my appetite."

At lunch time, she says, "You want a bowl of soup, or how about a plate of cheese and crackers, a glass of milk?"

He says, "No, thanks. It's the *Viagra*, it's really killed my appetite."

At dinner time, she says, "You want me to go buy us some burgers or a pizza, or make us a tasty stir-fry? That'd only take a couple of minutes."

He says, "Thanks, but the damn *Viagra* has totally chased my appetite."

She says, "Well, would you mind getting the fuck *off* me? I'm *starving*."

|||||||||||||||||||||

The wife's in bed with the lover when they hear the husband pull into the driveway.

She says, "Go stand in the corner."

She covers him with talcum powder and says, "Pretend you're a statue."

Her husband walks into the bedroom, sees the guy and says, "Who's that?"

She says, "It's a statue. I was at Smiths the other day and they have a statue, so I thought we should have a statue too."

He says, "All right."

They go to bed, and in the middle of the night the husband gets up, goes to the kitchen, makes a ham sandwich, grabs a Coca-Cola, comes back into the bedroom, hands it to the statue, and says, "Here, have this. I stood like that at Smiths for eight hours and nobody gave me nothin'."

|||||||||||||||||||||

A little old lady's very constipated so she goes to the doctor.

She says, "Doctor Schneiderman, it's simply terrible. I haven't had a crap in a week."

The doctor says, "Have you done anything about it?"

She says, "Well, of *course* I have. I sit in the bathroom for a half-hour in the morning, and then again for another half-hour at night."

The doctor says, "No, no, no...I mean, do you *take* anything?"

She says, "Of *course* I do. I take a book."

||||||||||||||||||||||

What're the three biggest lies a cowboy tells?

The truck is paid for, I quit drinking, and I was just trying to help that sheep over the fence.

||||||||||||||||||||||

Here we are in Carnegie Hall, and the world's greatest hypnotist is on stage swinging a long chain with a watch on the end.

He's saying, "You're all in my power...*you're all in my power...*"

Fifteen hundred people are swaying back and forth...back and forth...

He's saying, "You're all in my...," when he accidentally drops the watch.

He says, "*Shit.*"

It took them *two weeks* to dig everybody out.

||||||||||||||||||||||

How do you rejuvenate an old hooker?

Put a fifteen-pound ham in her snatch and yank out the bone.

||||||||||||||||||||||

Whiteside's walking around Home Depot when he sees an old high school pal.

He says, "Walter? Is that you? I haven't seen you in thirty years. Man, you look great."

Walter says, "Yeah, it's me. Yeah, I take good care of myself. Work out, eat right, don't drink or smoke. What are you up to?"

Whiteside says, "Ah, my wife and I always get separated in these big stores. I'm trying to find her."

Walter says, "My wife's lost too."

Whiteside says, "We should go looking for them together. What's your wife look like?"

Walter says, "She's twenty-seven, long blonde hair, great body. What's your wife look like?"

Whiteside says, "Fuck it; let's look for yours."

|||||||||||||||||||||||||

There're two statues in the park, a male statue and a female statue, and they've been facing each other for hundreds of years. One day a bolt of lightning strikes them both and brings them to life. They look into each other's eyes and without saying a word, they run, meet each other halfway, join hands, and disappear into the woods. A half hour later, they come staggering out and they can hardly catch their breath.

The female statue looks at the male statue, smiles and says, "Let's rest up a while and then go in there and do it again."

The male statue says, "Okay, only this time, *you* hold the pigeons and *I'll* shit on them."

|||||||||||||||||||||||||

Two out-of-work actors meet on the street.

The first actor says, "I just got a day job as a bathroom attendant and man do I hate it. In the morning, the homos come in and it's blow jobs in the stalls. The semen and the condoms are flying— it's *disgusting*. Then in the afternoon, the drunks come in, and they throw up—there's puke everywhere—it's horrible. I'll tell you, yesterday a guy came in at six o'clock and took a shit...it was like a breath of fresh air."

IIIIIIIIIIIIIIIIIIIIIII

Dolenz says to his wife, "Were you faking it last night?"
She says, "No, I was really asleep."

SECTION TWELVE

Shop 'til You Drip

The third-grade teacher says, "Johnny, what do you want to do when you grow up?"

Johnny says, "When I grow up I wanna be really rich and have lots of stuff and my own plane and get a whore and travel all over the world getting' drunk and havin' a great frickin' time."

The teacher says, "Umm...*uhh*...v-very good, John. M-Mary, what do you want to do when you grow up?"

Mary says, "I wanna be Johnny's whore."

||||||||||||||||||||||

Why's it take so long to fuck your grandmother?

You have to search every nook and cranny in granny to find the cranny with the nookie.

||||||||||||||||||||||

It's the beginning of the Revolution and Paul Revere's on his famous ride.

He stops in front of a house and yells up, "*Hey, lady!* Is your husband home?"

A lady comes to the window and yells back, "*Yes.*"

He says, "Tell him the British are coming!"

He stops at the next house and yells up, "*Hey, lady!* Is your husband home?"

A lady comes to the window and yells back, "*Yes.*"

He says, "Tell him the British are coming!"

He stops at the next house and yells up, "*Hey, lady!* Is your husband home?"

A lady comes to the window and yells back, "*No.*"

He goes, "*Whoooaaa!*"

||||||||||||||||||||||

A couple gets married and the maid of honor dances with the groom to the first song. And then they dance the second song, and the third. By the time they start dancing to the fourth song, the bride's pissed. She runs up and kicks her new husband between the legs. It starts a huge fight and soon the bride and the groom and all of the guests are hauled off to jail.

In court the next day, the judge says to the maid of honor, "What happened?"

She says, "Your honor, we were just dancing, and that crazy witch ran up and kicked her new husband in the balls."

The judge says, "*Yowch*. That must have *hurt*."

She says, "Well, fuck *yeah*. She broke three of my fingers."

|||||||||||||||||||||||||

Dirty Johnny walks into a luncheonette and orders a cup of coffee.

The waitress sets it down in front of him and Johnny says, "P-I-S-S."

She says, "You little *pig*. Get out of here."

Johnny gets up, and as he's going out the door he turns and says, "C-U-N-T."

She screams, a cop outside hears her, he grabs Johnny, the waitress explains, and the cop takes Johnny to the station house and puts him in front of the judge.

The judge says, "Son, according to the report, you ordered coffee, and when the waitress served you, you said to her, 'P-I-S-S.'"

Johnny says, "That's right, Judge. All I meant was, 'Put in some sugar.'"

The judge smiles slightly, and then says, "But what did you mean when you were leaving and you said, 'C-U-N-T'?"

Johnny says, "Your honor, all I meant was, 'See you next Thursday.'"

The judge laughs and says, "Heh, heh, heh. Case dismissed."

Johnny gets up, and as he's walking out the courtroom door, he turns and says, "By the way, your honor, F-U-C-K Y-O-U."

The judge says, "Hah, hah, hah. What's *that* mean?"

Johnny says, "*Fuck you!*"

||||||||||||||||||||||||

What'd the Seven Dwarfs say when Snow White woke up from her deep sleep?

"*I guess it's back to jerking off.*"

||||||||||||||||||||||||

Mack and Jamie are out hiking when they get chased by a bear. They scurry up a tree and the bear starts climbing up after them. Mack reaches in his backpack, takes out his running shoes, and starts putting them on.

Jamie says, "What are you doing?"

Mack says, "Well, I figure when the bear gets up close to us, we'll jump down and make a run for it."

Jamie says, "What are you, *stupid?* You can't outrun a *bear.*"

Mack says, "I don't have to outrun the *bear.* I just have to outrun *you.*"

||||||||||||||||||||||||

A priest's getting a flat tire fixed.

As the car's coming down on the lift, the priest says to the mechanic, "Are those lug nuts tight?"

The mechanic says, "Tight as a nun's cunt, Father."

The priest says, "Then you better give 'em another turn."

||||||||||||||||||||||

After an exam, the doctor says, "Jesus *Christ*, Allman. You've totally overdone it with your sex life. You've *completely* burnt yourself out. You know what you've got left? For the rest of your life, you've got fourteen orgasms. *Fourteen orgasms*, that's it."

Allman goes home and tells his wife the news.

She says, "Oh, no. Well, we'd better make a list of when you're going to use them."

He says, "I already did. *You* ain't on it."

||||||||||||||||||||||

Wolanin's in San Francisco when he suddenly gets terrible stomach pains. He goes to a local doctor and the doctor orders an emergency colonoscopy. Wolanin's naked on his side as the beautiful nurse starts the procedure.

The nurse says, "Please don't be concerned—at this stage of the procedure it's quite normal to get an erection."

Wolanin says, "I haven't got an erection."

The nurse says, "I know, but I do."

||||||||||||||||||||||

A kid's on a stoop crying.

A priest comes along and says, "What's the matter, son?"

The kid says, "My dog died."

The priest says, "Don't worry, he's with God now."

The kid says, "What the fuck's God want with a dead dog?"

||||||||||||||||||||||

A blonde's swerving down the road and gets pulled over by a cop.
He looks at her license and says, "Are you a natural blonde?"
She says, "Yeah."
The cop tosses his ticket book and starts pulling down his zipper.
She says, "Oh, no...not another *Breathalyzer* test."

||||||||||||||||||||||

Ten Catholic priests are killed in a car accident.
At the Pearly Gates, St. Peter says, "If any of you are pedophiles, please get out of this line and go straight to Hell."
Nine of them turn and start to walk away.
St. Peter says, "And take this deaf cocksucker with you."

||||||||||||||||||||||

A cop pulls a guy over and says, "Have you been drinking?"
The guy says, "Wh-why? I-is there a big fat pig sitting next to me?"

||||||||||||||||||||||

Snyder's wife dies. The pallbearers are carrying the casket, and as they start down some steps, the casket accidentally *bumps!* the wall and they hear, "*Unhh!*"
They open it up and she's still alive! She lives ten more years, and then she dies again. The same funeral parlor, the same pallbearers.
As they start down the stairs, Snyder says, "Be *careful* of the fucking *wall.*"

||||||||||||||||||||||

Stern walks into Barnes & Noble and says to the girl behind the counter, "Do you have the new book for men with short penises? I can't remember the title."

She says, "I don't think it's in yet."

Stern says, "That's it. I'll take one."

||||||||||||||||||||||

A big fat lady pushes her car into a gas station.

The mechanic says, "What's the matter?"

She says, "It conked out."

He opens the hood and in a few minutes, it's purring like a kitten.

She says, "What's the story?"

He says, "Crap in the carburetor."

She says, "How often do I have to do *that*?"

||||||||||||||||||||||

What're the two most important holes in your mom?

Her nostrils, so she can breathe between squirts.

||||||||||||||||||||||

Harry and Charlie are swapping stories.

Harry says, "One time during the war I was captured and held for weeks without food."

Charlie says, "How'd you survive without food?"

Harry says, "It was rough, but I had a big meal before I was captured and learned to eat my own shit."

Charlie says, "*What?* That's disgusting. I don't believe you."

Harry reaches into his pants, shits a bit in his hand, and eats it.

Charlie says, "My God. You're a *freak*. We can bet big money and rake in a fortune."

Harry says, "Sounds good to me. I could use the money."

The next day Charlie sets up a bet with two local gamblers.

The first gambler says, "This I gotta see. Nobody can eat their own shit."

Charlie sets down a plate full of shit in front Harry. Harry looks down and gets all ready to dig in when, all of a sudden, he jumps up from the table, and pukes all over the two gamblers. In a rage, the gamblers beat the hell out of Harry and Charlie, take their winnings, and leave.

Charlie says, "We lost it all. Why didn't you eat the shit?"

Harry says, "There was a hair in it."

||||||||||||||||||||||

Burford lives alone on a remote island. One day as he's riding his horse along the beach he sees a beautiful woman standing at an easel painting the ocean. He rides up and down in front of her, but she doesn't react to him at all.

He says to himself, "I'll paint my horse yellow, and then she'll notice me. She'll say, 'Oh, I see you have a yellow horse.' And I'll get talking to her, and then I'll invite her back to my cabin for lunch, and we'll have a bottle of wine, and then I'll open another bottle and we'll talk some more, and then it'll start to get cold, so I'll light a fire, and we'll be sitting close in front of it...soon we'll gently touch, then kiss, then make beautiful love all night long...yeah, that's what I'll do."

So he paints his horse yellow and rides down the beach.

The lady looks up and says, "I see you have a yellow horse."

Burford says, "Yeah. Can I fuck you?"

||||||||||||||||||||||

Sophie was a child actor. Now she's forty-five, five-foot-two, a hundred and eighty pounds, and has been divorced three times.

She says, "Ma, Bernie and Irving both want to marry me. Who will be the lucky one?"

Her mother says, "The *truth*? I think Bernie will marry you, and Irving will be the lucky one."

|||||||||||||||||||||||

Berman and Ellis are drinking, and after a couple of hours Berman leans over and starts stroking Ellis's beard.

He says, "You know, your face feels just like my wife's pussy."

Ellis reaches up, strokes his beard, and says, "You know, you're right."

|||||||||||||||||||||||

A Fed Ex guy knocks on the door. The door opens and there's a little kid, naked except for his underpants. He's smoking a joint and in the other hand he has a half-full bottle of Jack Daniels.

The Fed Ex guy says, "Kid, is your mother home?"

The kid says, "What do *you* think?"

|||||||||||||||||||||||

Rosegarten's duck won't eat, so he takes it to a vet.

The vet says, "When ducks get old, their upper bills grow down over their lower bills and make it hard for them to pick up food. You need to file down his upper bill even with his lower bill. But be careful, because a duck's nostrils are in his upper bill and if you file it down too much, when he takes a drink of water he'll drown."

A week later the doctor runs into Rosegarten and says, "So how's your duck?"

Rosegarten says, "He's dead."

The doctor says, "*Dead?* Jesus, man, I told you not to file his upper bill down too far. So he took a drink of water and drowned?"

Rosegarten says, "No, I think he was dead before I took him out of the vise."

||||||||||||||||||||||

A little old lady goes into the doctor's office and says, "M-my husband's having a hell of a time s-satisfying me. He's having trouble g-getting a hard-on."

The doctor says, "How old is your husband, ma'am?"

She says, "Eighty-s-six."

The doctor says, "*Eighty-six?* Well, I can certainly understand him having a bit of trouble. When did it happen?"

She says, "Tw-twice last night a-and once this morning."

||||||||||||||||||||||

Newman's standing at the bar and he's got two huge lumps on his head.

The bartender says, "I gotta ask, pal...what the hell happened to you?"

Newman says, "My wife hit me with a chair."

The bartender says, "Why the hell'd she do that?"

Newman says, "Well, I guess I earned it. She brought home a do-it-yourself waxing kit this morning and asked me if she should just do the sides and leave a strip down the middle. And I said I'd prefer she have no moustache at all."

||||||||||||||||||||||

What goes "*Click click click*...did I get it? *Click click click*...did I get it?"

That's Helen Keller doing the Rubik's cube.

|||||||||||||||||||||||

A woman's in labor, up in the stirrups, and she's cursing and screaming at her husband.

He says, "Hey, don't blame me. I wanted to stick it in your ass, but you said, 'No, that'll hurt.'"

|||||||||||||||||||||||

A lady in a bar says to the guy next to her, "I see you drink beer."

"Yep."

"How many a day?"

"Usually about three."

"And how much do you pay for a beer?"

"About six bucks, including the tip."

"And how long have you been drinking?"

"About twenty years, I suppose."

"So a beer costs six dollars and you have three beers a day, which puts your spending each month well over five hundred dollars."

"I guess."

"If in one year you spend six thousand dollars, in the past twenty years you've spent a hundred and twenty thousand dollars on beer."

"Your math sounds about right."

"Do you realize that if you didn't drink beer, that money could have been put in a savings account, and after twenty years of compound interest you could have bought a Ferrari?"

"Do you drink beer?"

"No."

"Where's *your* fucking Ferrari?"

140

||||||||||||||||||||||

What would you call a hooker with jizz all over her face?
Call her a taxi—her job is done.

SECTION THIRTEEN

'til Death Do US a Favor

Bernstein's out to dinner with his wife to celebrate her fortieth birthday.

He says, "So what would you like, Julie? A Jaguar? A sable coat? A diamond necklace?"

She says, "I want a divorce."

He says, "I wasn't planning on spending that much."

|||||||||||||||||||||

A guy's in a taxi on the way home from a business trip a day early.

It's after midnight and he says, "Cabbie, I think my wife's been cheating on me. If I give you a thousand bucks, will you be my witness?"

The cabbie says, "Sure, pal."

They get to the house, go in very quietly, the husband grabs his gun from the closet, and he and the cabbie tip-toe upstairs. The husband pushes open the bedroom door, switches on the light, pulls the blanket off, and seeing his wife and a stranger lying there naked, he puts the gun to the naked guy's head.

His wife says, *"Don't do it*, Harry! I lied when I told you I inherited money. Felix paid for the Corvette I gave you, he paid for the cabin cruiser, and he paid for our country club membership. Felix even pays our monthly club dues."

The husband lowers the gun and says to the cabbie, "What would *you* do?"

The cabbie says, "I'd cover him with that blanket before Felix catches cold."

|||||||||||||||||||||

Two old guys are sitting on a bench and the first guy says, "I-I'm nothing but aches and pains, aches and pains. Y-you're about the same age as me, h-how do you feel?"

The second old guy says, "I-I feel like a newborn baby."

The first old guy says, "A newborn baby?"

The second old guy says. "Yeah, a newborn baby. I-I got no teeth, no hair, and I don't do nothing all day but shit in my pants."

|||||||||||||||||||||||

What's worse than sitting on Santa's lap and him getting an erection?

He gets up and you don't fall off.

|||||||||||||||||||||||

Feldman and his wife are watching a documentary about Alzheimer's when she says, "What a horrible condition that is. If I ever get Alzheimer's, I think I'll just shoot myself."

Feldman says, "You said that five minutes ago."

|||||||||||||||||||||||

Mrs. O'Rourke says, "Father McGuirk, me husband's dead."

The priest says, "Dead, is he, Mary? Did he have any last requests?"

She says, "That he did, Father. He said, 'Mary, please put down the fookin' gun.'"

|||||||||||||||||||||||

Loughran's mother's lonely, so he has the local pet store owner import and send her a South American macaw that can speak seven languages.

A few weeks later, Loughran calls his mother and says, "Mom, did you get a delivery from me?"

She says, "Yes, thank you so much, it was *delicious*."

Loughran says, "*Ma!* You *ate* it? Ma, that bird could speak *seven languages.*"

She says, "So why didn't he say something?"

||||||||||||||||||||||||

A waiter walks past a lady's table and he's digging away at his ass. She says, "*Waiter!* Have you got hemorrhoids?"

He says, "Just what's on the menu, lady."

||||||||||||||||||||||||

It's Christmas morning and Dirty Johnny's sitting on the floor, unwrapping his presents. His father's wearing nothing but a short bathrobe and he stands in front of Johnny and then bends way over to reach for a present.

Johnny looks up and says, "Hey, Pop, who gets the bagpipes?"

||||||||||||||||||||||||

Scott brings Patti Ann home after their first date. He parks the car in front of her house, takes out his prick, and puts it in her hand.

She screams, "I've got two words for you! *Drop dead!*"

She gets out of the car, *slams!* the door, runs up the walk, goes into her house, *slams!* the door, runs up into her room, and *slams!* the door. A few seconds later there's a knock on the door. She opens it up and there's Scott.

He says, "And I've got two words for you! *Let go!*"

||||||||||||||||||||||||

Freiberger's in a rest home. He goes into a bathroom stall, sits for fifteen minutes, and nothing happens. He's grunting and pushing, but nothing happens.

Feinman walks in, goes into the other stall, and right away Freiberger hears, "*Plooop!*"

Freiberger says, "You sure are lucky."

Feinman says, "*Lucky?* That was my *watch*."

||||||||||||||||||||||||||

A tall, handsome Polish kid's working in a supermarket and he's helping a middle-aged divorcee with her groceries.

When they get to the parking lot, she looks him up and down, smiles at him, and says, "I've got an itchy pussy."

He says, "Well, you better point it out, lady. All them Japanese cars look the same to me."

||||||||||||||||||||||||||

Did you hear about the Jewish car accident?

There was no damage to the car, but fortunately, everybody inside was hurt.

||||||||||||||||||||||||||

A honeymooning couple's driving along in the country. They stop by a pasture and they're leaning on the fence, looking out at a herd of cows.

All of a sudden, a bull comes over the rise, and *bang! bang! bang!* the bull fucks seven cows, right in a row. And when he gets done with the seventh one, he starts back at the beginning and fucks them all again.

The girl turns to her new husband and says, "You know, it's a shame a man can't perform like that."

He says, "We could— if you let us change cows every time."

|||||||||||||||||||||

The third-grade teacher says, "Class, today I want you to use the word "beautiful" in a sentence. Okay, Mary."

Mary says, "Teacher, I think you're beautiful."

The teacher says, "Oh, thank you, Mary. Very good. Claude?"

Claude says, "Um, teacher, I think the blue sky is beautiful."

The teacher says, "Very good, Claude."

Dirty Johnny stands up in back and says, "Yo, teach! I'll give it a shot."

The teacher says, "All right, John, go ahead."

Johnny says, "Last night at the dinner table, my sister said, 'Pop, I'm pregnant.' And he said, 'Beautiful. Fucking *beautiful.*'"

|||||||||||||||||||||

An old woman's standing at the bar when an old guy comes up and says, "C-can I buy you a drink?"

She says, "I-I'd like that."

A few minutes later he says, "C-can I buy you another drink?"

She says, "I-I'd like that."

As they're drinking, he puts his arm around her and starts snuggling her, and after a while he says, "W-would you like to come back to my place?"

She says, "I-I'd like that."

They're walking along hand-in-hand when she says, "I-I think I should tell you, I've got arthritis."

He says, "What, we're *old*, a little arthritis? A little arthritis doesn't bother *me*."

When they get to his house, they sit on the couch, and in no time they're French kissing, giving each other hickeys, he's got his hand up her back and undoes her bra with one hand like a good eighth-grader...she pulls down his zipper, he's fingering her...in no time at all these two old timers are on the floor naked. He goes down on her. And it's *horrible*.

He looks up and says, "Wh-what the hell's going on down here? It smells terrible."

She says, "Well, I-I told you on the way over here, I have arthritis."

He says, "I-is that what arthritis smells like down here?"

She says, "No, I-I've got it in my shoulder. I-I can't wipe my ass."

||||||||||||||||||||||||

Why'd God create women?
To carry the semen from the bedroom to the toilet.

||||||||||||||||||||||||

The morning after the high school prom, a woman gets a text from her daughter: "Mom, I'm freaking out. I got drunk, I'm at the beach, and I got cum in my hair."

Her mother texts back, "I'm really glad you're so open with me. Very often a guy will pull it out of your mouth to shoot on your face and some of it gets in your hair. Just jump in the water; it'll wash right out."

The girl texts back, "Thanks so much for sharing, Mom...but I meant to type *gum*."

||||||||||||||||||||||||

I was in a restaurant the other night and I saw two priests having dinner.

I didn't know whether to send over a bottle of wine or a Cub Scout.

IIIIIIIIIIIIIIIIIIIIIIIII

Burrow walks into the patent office and says to the girl behind the desk, "I'd like to register my new invention, a folding bottle."

She says, "Sure. What do you call it?"

He says, "A fottle."

She says, "That's kind of silly."

He says, "I'll work on the name. I also have a folding carton."

She says, "Okay. What do you call that?"

He says, "A farton."

She says, "That's rude. You can't even use that name."

He says, "I guess I'll scratch out the name for my folding bucket."

IIIIIIIIIIIIIIIIIIIIIIIII

Two girls are at the water cooler and the first one says, "I've got a terrible sore throat."

The second girl says, "Whenever I have a sore throat, I just go home and give my husband a blow job and it clears it right up. You should try it."

The next day they're at the water cooler again.

The second girl says, "I tried it and it worked like a charm. You know, your husband couldn't be*lieve* it was your idea."

IIIIIIIIIIIIIIIIIIIIIIIII

Mrs. Pascucci walks into an eye clinic and puts a big jar on the receptionist's desk. In the jar's a huge turd, fourteen inches long and five inches around.

She says to the receptionist, "I need to see an optometrist."

She says, "Ma'am, looking at the specimen in that jar, I'd say you need to see a *proctologist*, not an optometrist."

Mrs. Pascucci says, "No, I need to see an *optometrist*. Every time I take a shit, my eyes water."

||||||||||||||||||||||

Two girls are talking and the first one says, "I just read that it's against the law to go topless in the New York subways."

Her friend says, "Thank God. It's bad enough when you catch your *scarf* in those doors."

||||||||||||||||||||||

Two Chinese guys are playing golf and the first guy hits a great drive.

The second guy says, "Nice tee shot."

The first guy says, "Sank you velly velly much, my wife buy for me. Fit nice."

||||||||||||||||||||||

It's Saturday morning, Grillo's home alone, and there's a knock on the door. He answers it and there's a guy standing there.

The guy says, "Hello. I'm a Jehovah's Witness, and I have stories to tell you."

Grillo says, "Well, come on in."

Grillo shows him into the living room and says, "Let me get you a cup of coffee."

He gets the guy a cup of coffee and then says, "Now, what are these stories you have to tell me?"

The Jehovah's Witness says, "How the fuck should *I* know? I never got this far before."

||||||||||||||||||||||

A girl calls the priest.

She says, "Father, is it a sin to have sex before communion?"

He says, "Only if you block the aisle."

IIIIIIIIIIIIIIIIIIIIIIII

O'Toole gets a job working at the morgue.

His first day he comes up the stairs and says, "Boss, you've got to come downstairs. There's a problem with Mrs. McGruder. By God, there's a jumbo shrimp sticking right out of her snatch."

The boss says, "You're crazy."

He says, "I'm telling you, Mrs. McGruder's got a jumbo shrimp sticking right out of her snatch."

They go downstairs, the boss pulls back the sheet, and says, "You *jerk*. That's not a shrimp. That's her *clit*."

He says, "Well, it *tasted* like shrimp."

IIIIIIIIIIIIIIIIIIIIIIII

A drunk's walking down the sidewalk and there's two nuns coming the other way. At the last minute, the two nuns walk around either side of him.

He says, "H-how the hell'd she do *that*?"

IIIIIIIIIIIIIIIIIIIIIIII

A guy goes into a library and says to the librarian, "I need a book on suicide."

She says, "Fuck you. You won't bring it back."

IIIIIIIIIIIIIIIIIIIIIIII

A guy asks a Jewish girl to marry him.
She says no and he lives happily ever after.

|||||||||||||||||||||||

Youngman goes into the doctor's office for an examination.

The doctor says, "My *God*, man, there's a piece of lettuce sticking out of your ass."

Youngman says, "Doc, that's just the *tip* of the iceberg."

|||||||||||||||||||||||

What's the difference between a man and a hog?
A hog won't stay up and drink all night just so he can fuck a hog.

|||||||||||||||||||||||

A guy catches his kid jerking off.

He says, "Son, don't do that; you'll go blind."

The kid says, "Pop, I'm *over here*."

JACKIE MARTLING

SECTION FOURTEEN

The Stiff Dick of the Law

The cops show up at the house. There's a guy lying in a pool of blood and a woman holding a bloody 5-iron.

One of the cops says, "Is that your husband?"

"Yep."

"He's dead."

"Yep."

"Did you hit him with the golf club?"

"Yep."

"How many times?"

"I don't know. Four, five...put me down for four."

||||||||||||||||||||||

A blonde *smashes!* her car into a wall.

A cop comes up and says, "What happened?"

She says, "I was driving down the road when a tree jumped out in front of me. I swerved to avoid it, and there was another tree. I swerved to avoid it, and there was another tree. I swerved to avoid it, and I hit the wall."

The cop says, "Lady, there's no trees on this road for ten miles. That was your fucking *air freshener.*"

||||||||||||||||||||||

What would you call a guy with no arms and no legs, in a box with his arms and legs?

Kit.

||||||||||||||||||||||

Artie says to Danny, "My wife's making me crazy, I gotta get rid of her. But I'm afraid if I kill her I'll get caught."

Danny says, "There's a simple solution. Just fuck her to death. Fuck her five, six, seven times a day, and she'll be dead in six months."

Five months later Danny goes to see Artie and when he gets to the house he sees the yard's immaculate, there's music blaring from a speaker in the window, and Artie's wife is dancing spryly as she's tending to her huge vegetable and flower beds. He walks up to the porch, and there's Artie in a rocking chair. He's gaunt as hell, he weighs about ninety pounds, and he looks terrible.

Danny says, "Damn, Artie, your wife sure looks happy."

Artie says, "Y-yeah...l-little does she know she's only g-got three weeks to l-live."

|||||||||||||||||||||||||

What's the difference between a lawyer and a vagina?
You never feel like choking a vagina to death.

|||||||||||||||||||||||||

Balatsos says to the bartender, "I gotta get a divorce. I gotta have something different. I'm sick of the same old hole, every night. Every night, the same hole, the same hole, *the same hole.*"

The bartender says, "Why don't you just roll her over and use the other hole?"

Balatsos says, "What...and have all those fucking *kids* running around?"

|||||||||||||||||||||||||

What do you call it when a man has sex with three women at the racetrack?
A trifuckter.

Bartlett's always farting as loud as he can in bed and it's driving his poor wife crazy.

She says, "Bartlett, one of these times you're gonna be sorry. One of these nights you're going to blow your guts out."

The next afternoon Mrs. Bartlett's in the butcher shop, sees some chicken livers on sale, and gets an idea. She buys a pound of the chicken livers, then goes home and hides them under the bed. That night, she waits until Bartlett blasts away a few times. Then she reaches under the bed, grabs a handful of chicken livers, and throws them between the sheets.

She jumps up and screams, "God *damn* it, Bartlett, *look!* Look what you've done!"

Bartlett sees the livers, scoops them up, and runs into the bathroom. A few minutes later, he staggers out, looking really shaky.

His wife says, "I told you one day you were gonna blow your guts out!"

Bartlett lifts one of his hands and says, "Yep. And if it weren't for the grace of God and these two fingers, I'd have never got 'em back in again."

||||||||||||||||||||||

A kid walks in and says, "Mommy, I had sex with my teacher after school today."

She says, "You go sit in the corner until your father gets home."

He says, "I can't."

||||||||||||||||||||||

The Sunday School teacher says, "Can anybody tell me what the resurrection is?"

Dirty Johnny says, "I got no idea, I just know if it lasts more than four hours you gotta go to the hospital."

||||||||||||||||||||||||

Gooch gets on an elevator with a big fat broad.
He says, "Can I smell your snatch?"
She says, "*No.*"
He says, "Then it must be your feet."

||||||||||||||||||||||||

A marriage counselor says to the husband, "Say something to your wife that'll make her happy and sad at the same time."
He says, "For a fat pig, you don't sweat that much."
The marriage counselor says to the wife, "Uhh...*umm*...s-say something to your husband that'll make him happy and sad at the same time."
She says, "You've got a much bigger cock than your brother."

||||||||||||||||||||||||

Why do they bury Jewish guys standing up?
So the change won't fall out of their pockets.

||||||||||||||||||||||||

Messina's got two daughters and he wants a son. His wife gets pregnant and she has a boy. He's so excited, he rushes to the hospital, into the maternity ward, and it's the ugliest baby he's ever seen.
He says, "This is crazy. I've got two beautiful daughters."
He turns to his wife and says, "Have you been cheating on me?"
She says, "Not this time."

||||||||||||||||||||||

A midget walks into a bar, climbs up on a bar stool, and says, "Gimme a quadruple Jack Daniels."

The bartender gives him a quadruple Jack Daniels.

The midget says, "Who's the toughest guy in the bar tonight?"

The bartender says, "That guy down at the very end of the bar's pretty tough."

The midget says, "I'm gonna drink my drink and then go down there and kick his ass."

He drinks his drink, climbs down off the stool, beats the hell out of the guy, and leaves.

The next night, the midget walks into the bar again, climbs up on a bar stool, and says, "Gimme a quadruple Jack Daniels."

The bartender gives him a quadruple Jack Daniels.

The midget says, "Who's the toughest guy in the bar tonight?"

The bartender says, "That guy at the table in the checked shirt's pretty tough."

The midget says, "I'm gonna drink my drink and then go over there and kick his ass."

He drinks his drink, climbs down off the stool, beats the hell out of the guy, and leaves.

The bartender's pal says, "That midget's gonna wreck your business. We better do something."

The next day they go to the zoo, rent a gorilla, and put it in the bar's men's room.

That night, the midget walks into a bar, climbs up on a bar stool and says, "Gimme a quadruple Jack Daniels."

The bartender gives him a quadruple Jack Daniels.

The midget says, "Who's the toughest guy in the bar tonight?"

The bartender says, "He's waiting for you in the bathroom."

The midget says, "I'm gonna drink my drink and then go in there and kick his ass."

He drinks his drink, climbs down off the stool, goes into the bathroom, there's *crashing!* sounds, the walls are being pounded, glass is *smashing!*, and finally the midget comes walking out.

As he strolls past the bartender he says, "When that Italian broad comes to, tell her I threw her fur coat in the garbage can."

|||||||||||||||||||||||

Cooney goes to the doctor for an examination, and when it's done, the doctor says, "Mr. Cooney, you have an incurable disease. There's nothing I can do."

Cooney says, "Do you have any advice for me at all, Doc?"

The doctor says, "Take three mud baths a day."

Cooney says, "Will that make me live longer?"

The doctor says, "No, but it'll get you used to the dirt."

|||||||||||||||||||||||

How do you know when your ass is too hairy?
You take a shit and you don't hear a splash.

|||||||||||||||||||||||

An old guy's in a doctor's waiting room and says to the guy sitting next to him, "Why're you here?"

The second guy says, "I-I-I h-h-have a pr-pr-pretty bad st-st-stuttering problem. Wh-wh-why are y-y-you h-h-here?"

The old guy says, "I have a bad prostate."

The stutterer says, "Wh-wh-what's does th-th-that mean?"

The old guy says, "I piss like you talk."

IIIIIIIIIIIIIIIIIIIIIII

A kid from Australia comes to New York, meets a hooker, and she takes him to a hotel room. She takes off her shirt and the kid throws a chair out of the window. She takes off her pants and the kid throws the bed out of the window.

The hooker says, "Hey, smiley, you got any idea what we're gonna do in here?"

The kid says, "I think I *do*, ma'am, and if it's anything like it is with a kangaroo, we're gonna be needin' all the room we can get."

IIIIIIIIIIIIIIIIIIIIIII

Campbell goes to in to see a psychiatrist.

He says, "Doc, every morning when I wake up I have this irrepressible urge to stuff my nostrils full of tobacco."

The psychiatrist says, "You want a light?"

IIIIIIIIIIIIIIIIIIIIIII

Epstein's been shipwrecked on a desert island since he was eight years old and hasn't seen another human being for more than twenty years. One day, walking along the beach, he comes across a beautiful blonde girl lying nude on the beach, the victim of another shipwreck, and he tells her his story.

She says, "How have you survived here alone for all this time?"

Epstein says, "I fish, I gather berries and coconuts and fruit, and I dig for clams."

She says, "What about fucking?"

Epstein says, "*Fucking?* What's *that?*"

She shows him...and shows him...and shows him...and then she shows him one last time.

When they're finally done, she says, "Well, how do you like fucking?"

Epstein says, "I-I guess it's all right. But look what you did to my *clam digger.*"

||||||||||||||||||||||

Halvangis is walking up to go in for his army physical and there's a nun outside the building.

He grovels at her feet, wraps his arms around her leg, and says, "You gotta help me, sister. I can't carry a gun. I can't shoot anybody. I can't fight in a war."

She says, "Reach up under my habit and you'll feel balls. I ain't going to Vietnam either."

||||||||||||||||||||||

A couple's lying in bed and the husband says, "Let's play a game."

He cuts a big fart, *Lbbt!*, and says, "Seven points, I'm winning."

His wife lifts her leg and farts, *Lbbt!*, and she says, "That's seven for me?"

He says, "Yep."

He strains, squeezes out another one, *Lbbt!*, and he says, "Fourteen to seven."

She farts again, *Lbbt!*, and says, "That ties it up?"

He says, "Yep," and then he pushes really hard and shits the bed.

She says, "Now what?"

He says, "Halftime, switch sides."

||||||||||||||||||||||

Sheilah Schwartz is forty years old and her mother's freaking out that Sheilah's not married, so she sends her on a cruise around the world. Three months later, Sheilah walks in the front door followed

161

by a huge black man. He's naked except for a grass skirt and a shark tooth necklace, and he's got a bone through his nose.

Sheila's mother says, "*Oy*, Sheilah...I told you to bring home a *rich* doctor, not a *witch* doctor."

||||||||||||||||||||||||

What would you call a Japanese prizefighter whose father has diarrhea?

A slap-happy Jappy with a crap-happy pappy.

||||||||||||||||||||||||

Shire's in a taxi when he leans forward and taps the driver on the shoulder. The driver screams, loses control, the car leaps over the curb, and it *smashes!* into a lamppost.

Shire says, "Jeez, I didn't mean to *startle* you. I just wanted to ask you something."

The driver says "It's not your fault, pal. This is my first day driving a cab. For the last twenty-five years I drove a hearse."

||||||||||||||||||||||||

A college couple's under a tree making out.

The girl says, "Tommy, I wish you had a flashlight."

He says, "Why's that?"

She says, "Because you've been eating grass for fifteen minutes."

||||||||||||||||||||||||

A guy gets a new job, so to celebrate he goes and buys himself a brand-new suit and a pair of shiny, new, black patent leather shoes. Then he decides to go dancing.

He asks a girl to dance, looks down, looks back at her, and says, "I like a girl who wears polka-dot panties."

She says, "How do you know I'm wearing polka-dot panties?"

He says, "I saw the reflection in my shiny, new, black patent leather shoes."

He asks another girl to dance, looks down, looks back at her, and says, "I like a girl who wears striped undies."

She says, "How do you know I'm wearing striped undies?"

He says, "I saw the reflection in my shiny, new, black patent leather shoes."

He asks another girl to dance. He looks down, looks back at her...then he looks down, looks back at her.

He says, "What do you got on under that dress?"

She says, "Nothin'."

He says, "*Whew.* I thought I had a *crack* in my shiny, new, black patent leather shoes."

|||||||||||||||||||||||

A drunk's walking along when a guy coming the other way says, "Why're you walking with one foot up on the curb and one foot on the road?"

The drunk says, "Th-thank God. I-I thought I was cripple."

|||||||||||||||||||||||

Haberman's playing a round of golf with three new guys. He tees up his ball, swings, and completely misses. He swings again and misses again. He swings once more and completely misses the ball again.

He turns to the three guys and says, "Tough course."

|||||||||||||||||||||||

Reeb's on a plane and just as they're taking off, he sees the lady across the aisle from him who's breastfeeding. A few hours later they're coming in for a landing, and she's breastfeeding again.

He leans over and says, "Ma'am, I couldn't help notice that you were breastfeeding your baby on take-off and now you're breastfeeding again on landing. Is there a reason?"

She says, "Yes, I breastfeed my baby on take-off and landing so his ears won't pop."

He says, "*Fuck!* And all these years I've been chewing gum."

||||||||||||||||||||||

Mehrtens says, "Doc, you gotta help me. I got this uncontrollable urge to fuck horses."

The doctor says, "Male or female?"

Mehrtens says, "*Male*. I ain't no *queer*."

SECTION FIFTEEN

Horny Like a Reindeer

Dirty Johnny's parents take him to see Santa Claus and Johnny climbs up on Santa's knee.

Santa says, "What do you want for Christmas?"

He taps Johnny on the nose as he spells out, "Some *t-o-y-s*?"

Johnny taps Santa's nose the same way and says, "No, I've got lots of *t-o-y-s*."

Santa taps, "Do you want some *c-a-n-d-y*?"

Johnny taps back, "No, I got tons of stupid *c-a-n-d-y*."

Santa says, "Well, what do you want?"

Johnny taps on Santa's nose, "Some *p-u-s-s-y*, and I know you can get me some, because I smell it on your fingers."

|||||||||||||||||||||||

Three kids are talking about Christmas.

The first kid says, "My Pop hides the Christmas presents in the attic."

The second kid says, "My father hides the Christmas presents in the basement."

The third kid says, "My old man hides the Christmas presents in his pants."

The first kid says, "*What?*"

The third kid says, "Yeah. When I told my old man I wanted a bike for Christmas, he grabbed his crotch and said, 'I got your bike right here.'"

|||||||||||||||||||||||

Harry runs into Marty, who married Harry's ex-wife just months after they got divorced.

Harry says, "So Marty, how do you like that second-hand pussy?"

Marty says, "It's fine, once you get past that used part in the front."

||||||||||||||||||||||

Mrs. Siegel calls the hospital and says, "I'm going to sue you people. After my husband's surgery he lost all interest in sex."

The hospital spokesman says, "Lady, your husband was operated on for his cataracts. All we did was correct his eyesight."

||||||||||||||||||||||

A nun's sitting on a plane next to a priest and she's doing a crossword puzzle.

She says, "Father, what's a four-letter word ending in *u-n-t* that means a kind of woman?"

The priest says, "Aunt."

The nun says, "Have you got an eraser?"

||||||||||||||||||||||

Puscas goes up to a girl in a bar and says, "Hello. I'd like to get to know you better. I'm forty-eight years old, I've been a Congressman for ten years, and I'm honest."

She says, "Hi. I'm thirty years old, I've been a hooker for fifteen years, and I'm a virgin."

||||||||||||||||||||||

How many calories do you get from eating pussy?

It depends which direction she wipes her ass.

||||||||||||||||||||||

A nun and a priest are going across the desert on a camel when the camel drops dead. They try everything to revive it. They pound on his heart, give him mouth-to-mouth resuscitation, but the camel's as dead as a doornail.

The nun says, "Father, we're sure to die out here. Could you please do me a favor, Father? My entire life I've been in the convent, raised from birth to be a nun, and I've never seen what's between a man's legs. Could you help me, Father?"

Well, forget it, the priest can hardly get his pants down over his boner. He finally gets his them off and he's got a raging hard-on.

The nun looks at it and says, "My *God*, Father, what's *that*?"

The priest says "This, my child, is what gives life."

The nun says, "Well, then why don't you shove it up that camel's ass so we can get the fuck out of here?"

||||||||||||||||||||||

Mazzilli says, "Doc, I can't stop singing 'The Green, Green Grass of Home.'"

The doctor says, "That sounds like Tom Jones Syndrome."

Mazzilli says, "Is that common?"

The doctor says, "It's not unusual."

||||||||||||||||||||||

A drunk's walking out of a bar just as a lady comes walking up with her chihuahua. The drunk *stumbles!* and pukes all over the dog.

He looks down and says, "I-I don't remember eating that."

||||||||||||||||||||||

Porricelli's in line at the supermarket when a blonde at the back of the line starts waving to him.

He doesn't recognize her, so he walks over and says, "I'm sorry, do I know you?"

She says, "I may be mistaken, but I think you might be the father of one of my children."

He says, "Holy *shit*...a- are you the stripper from my bachelor party? It's foggy, but I kind of remember fucking you on the pool table in front of all the guys...didn't your girlfriend stick a cucumber up my ass?"

She says, "No, no, no...I think I'm your son's English teacher."

||||||||||||||||||||||||

Four businessmen eat every day in the same Chinese restaurant, and to pass the time, they do everything they can think of to torture the waiter.

One day one of them says, "L-look, we've been busting Chan's balls for a long time. I-I think it's time we straightened up."

Another one of them says, "Th-that's a good idea. H-hey, Hung Lo, c-come on over here."

The waiter comes over and says "Ooo-*ahh*-so. What can I do for you misters?"

The first guy says, "L-listen, I know we always give you a hard time, but things a-are going to change. From now on, w-we're gonna treat you good, a-and we're going to give you a good tip every day. What do you think of that?"

The waiter bows and says, "*Ahh!* Very good. Now I don't have to piss in your coffee."

||||||||||||||||||||||||

Friedman goes in to see a psychiatrist.

The psychiatrist says, "Mr. Friedman, what are you looking for in a woman?"

Friedman says, "Big tits."

The psychiatrist says, "No, I mean for a serious relationship."

Friedman says, "*Seriously* big tits."

The psychiatrist says, "No, no, no, *no*. I mean, what are you looking for in the one woman you'll be spending the rest of your life with?"

Friedman says, "No woman's got tits that big."

||||||||||||||||||||||

What's the difference between Santa Claus and a bartender?
Santa Claus only has to look at eight assholes.

||||||||||||||||||||||

Harry gets drunk and says to his wife, "Y-you're ugly."

She says, "That's so mean. Say you're sorry."

He says, "I-I'm sorry you're ugly."

||||||||||||||||||||||

Bennington's sitting on a train looking over at a lady with her baby and he says, "Lady, that's the ugliest baby I've ever seen. My God, what an ugly kid. That baby looks like a monkey."

The lady starts crying uncontrollably—she's really freaking out.

She runs up to the conductor and says, "That man over there insulted me. He's so mean. I'm so upset."

The conductor says, "Calm down, ma'am, calm down. Next stop we'll jump off and get you a nice hot cup of coffee. Hey, maybe we'll even find a banana for your monkey."

||||||||||||||||||||||

170

Why don't hens have tits?
Hey, it's hard enough to keep the farmers from fucking them as it is.

||||||||||||||||||||||

A mountain man comes down from the hills and sees a deserted cabin. On one wall of the cabin is a knothole about waist-high that's shaped a bit like a pussy. He looks around, pulls down his pants, and starts fucking it. After a few minutes, there's a tap on his shoulder. He turns around and there's a hillbilly standing there.

The hillbilly says, "Would y'all mind doin' that from the *inside*? My family's in there eatin' dinner."

||||||||||||||||||||||

Why'd God create midgets?
To give cripples something to laugh at.

||||||||||||||||||||||

Hawthorne's standing at a urinal when a black guy runs in and whips it out and starts pissing. He looks down, and the black guy's got a white cock.

Hawthorne says, "I didn't mean to stare, but I never saw a black guy with a white dick before."

The other guy says, "I'm not black. I'm a coal miner on my honeymoon."

||||||||||||||||||||||

Simone's in a small town in Mississippi on a business trip, goes into the local bar, and sits next to a redneck.

After a bunch of beers, Simone says, "Is it true you guys here in the South date your own cousins?"

The redneck says, "Well, *hell* no. That's a lie made up by people from the North just to poke fun at us. *Shiiiit*, I've lived down here all my life, and I ain't never dated none of my cousins. Oh, I fucked a few of them, but I ain't never took none of 'em nowhere."

||||||||||||||||||||||||

Nelson hires a clown for his kid's seventh birthday party.

The clown gets up in front of the kids, puts his hand in his pocket, and says, "If any of youse can guess what I got in my pocket, you win a prize."

A kid in the front says, "Is it candy, mister?"

The clown says, "No, it ain't candy."

Another kid says, "Is it *money*, mister?"

The clown says, "No, it ain't money, either."

Another kid says, "Well, what is it, then?"

The clown says, "It's my cock."

Nelson grabs the clown, drags him into the kitchen, and says, "What the hell was *that*? These kids are seven years old."

The clown says, "I'm sorry, all right? I'm really hungover and by accident I went into my nightclub act. Don't worry, I got it together now."

Nelson says, "You better, or I'll call the police. Now get back in there and entertain those kids. They all love you."

The clown gets back up in front of the kids and says, "Okay, kids, let's start all over again. If any of youse can guess what I got in my pocket, you win a prize."

A kid says, "Is it candy, mister?"

The clown says, "No, it ain't candy."

Another kid says, "Is it *money*, mister?"

The clown says, "No, it ain't money, either."

Another kid says, "Well, what is it, then?"

The clown looks over at Nelson and says, "You better call the cops. It's my cock again."

||||||||||||||||||||||

What's the difference between a beer and a booger?
You put your beer on top *of the table.*

||||||||||||||||||||||

The nurse in a mental institution walks into Charlie's room and he's pretending to be steering a car.

She says, "Charlie, what're you doing?"

He says, "I'm driving to Chicago."

She says, "Have a nice trip."

The next day she walks into Charlie's room just as he's stopping his imaginary car.

She says, "What's going on, Charlie?"

Charlie says, "I just got into Chicago."

She says, "Terrific."

She goes across the hall into Bob's room and he's sitting up in bed naked jerking wildly on his prick.

She says, "Bob, what're you *doing?*"

He says, "I'm fucking Charlie's wife while he's in Chicago."

||||||||||||||||||||||

It's a nasty day.

A lady midget walks into a doctor's office and says, "Doc, every time it rains, I get this terrible pain in my crotch."

He says, "Let's get you on my exam table and I'll see what I can do," and he helps her up.

In just a few minutes he says, "Okay, leap down."

She leaps down, and then says, "*Doc!* I feel *great!* What'd you do?"

He says, "I cut two inches off the tops of your galoshes."

||||||||||||||||||||||

Frawley's lying in his hospital bed when the doctor comes in and says, "Well, I've got good news and bad news."

Frawley says, "Give me the bad news first."

The doctor says, "We have to amputate both of your legs."

Frawley says, "My *God*. What's the good news?"

The doctor says, "The guy across the hall wants to buy your slippers."

||||||||||||||||||||||

Why're sperm shaped like tadpoles?
Because a woman would never swallow a frog.

||||||||||||||||||||||

A bunch of guys are in a golf club locker room when a cellphone on a bench rings. One of the guys is drying himself off and hits it onto speaker phone. Everybody else can't help but listen.

He says, "Hello?"

A woman says, "Honey, it's me. Are you at the club?"

He says, "Yeah."

She says, "I'm at the mall and I found a beautiful leather coat, and it's only a thousand dollars. Is it okay if I buy it?"

He says, "Sure, if you like it that much, go ahead."

She says, "And I stopped by the Mercedes dealership and saw a new 2018 model that I really liked."

He says, "How much?"

She says, "Ninety thousand dollars."

He says, "Okay, but for that price I want it with all the options."

She says, "Great. Oh, and one more thing...the house I wanted last year is back on the market. They're asking 950,000 dollars."

He says, "Well, then go ahead and give them an offer of 900,000 dollars. They'll probably take it. But, if not, we can go the extra fifty thousand."

She says, "Okay. I'll see you later. I love you so much."

He says, "I love you too."

He hangs up and then notices everybody's staring at him.

He smiles and says, "Any of you guys know whose phone this is?"

|||||||||||||||||||||||||

Lange walks into a crowded doctor's office and says to the receptionist, "There's something wrong with my cock."

The receptionist says, "You shouldn't use that language in the reception area. Please leave, and when you come back in, say there's something wrong with your ear, or something like that."

Lange walks out, walks back in, and the receptionist says, "Can I help you?"

Lange says, "There's something wrong with my ear."

The receptionist says, "And what's wrong with your ear?"

He says, "It burns like fuck when I piss out of it."

SECTION SIXTEEN

Pets with Benefits

Finn's wife keeps nagging him to take her hunting, so he finally agrees to take her hunting on Saturday.

Saturday comes, it's pouring rain, and she says, "I ain't going huntin' in the rain."

He says, "Oh, you're going hunting in the rain. You're going hunting in the rain, or I'm fucking you in the ass, or you're sucking my cock. Now make up your mind, I gotta go get the dogs ready."

When he comes back in she says, "I ain't going huntin' in the rain. And you sure as *hell* ain't fucking me in my ass, so I'll blow you."

She gets down on her knees, starts sucking his dick, and then she *spits!* and says, "*Yuckhh!* Your dick tastes like *shit*."

He says, "Yeah, the dogs didn't want to go hunting either."

||||||||||||||||||||||||

One day the wife's out and texts her husband, "If you're sleeping, send me your dreams...if you're laughing, send me your smile...if you're drinking, send me a sip..."

He texts back, "I'm taking a shit. Please advise."

||||||||||||||||||||||||

Paw yells out the window, "What're y'all doin' out there?"

Jethro yells back, "We's all fuckin' momma."

Paw yells, "Okay, just be sure t' stay away from them nasty cigarettes."

||||||||||||||||||||||||

A moth goes into a podiatrist's office.

The podiatrist says, "What's your problem?"

The moth says, "Neither of my parents loved me, I don't think any of my brothers and sisters even *like* me, and I have no friends."

The podiatrist says, "You don't need a podiatrist—you need a *psychiatrist*. Why'd you come in here?"

The moth says, "Because the light was on."

||||||||||||||||||||||

Weir's fucking a woman when they hear a car pull into the driveway.

She says, "That's my husband."

Weir says, "Where's the back door?"

She says, "We don't have a back door."

Weir says, "Where would you like one?"

||||||||||||||||||||||

A white couple's walking along and they see a black couple with their baby.

The white guy turns to his wife and says, "You know, we have six children of our own, but we've never been able to have a black child."

She says, "You know, I couldn't help but notice. Why don't you go over and ask them for some advice?"

He says, "That's a good idea."

He goes up to the black couple and says, "Your kid's so cute. Me and my wife, we've got six kids, but we've never been able to have a black child. Do you think you could give us some advice?"

The black guy holds his forefingers about twelve inches apart and says, "Well, is it about that long?"

The white guy says, "No, it's about like this," and he holds his fingers about two inches apart.

The black guy makes a big circle with both thumbs and forefingers and says, "Yeah? Well, is it about that big around?"

The white guy says, "No, it's like this," and he makes a small circle with his thumb and forefinger.

The black guy says, "That's the problem. You lettin' in too much light."

||||||||||||||||||||||

What's the definition of love?
That's when your heart melts and it comes squirting out of the end of your cock.

||||||||||||||||||||||

A farmer comes into town to go to the movies and he's got his pet goose with him.

He's about to go into the movie when the ticket taker says to him, "I'm sorry, sir; no pets allowed."

Well, he came all the way into town and he wants to see the movie, so he goes around the corner and sticks the goose down his pants. He comes back, hands the ticket taker his ticket, and goes in. Halfway through the movie, the goose starts jumping around in the farmer's pants, so he pulls down his zipper so the goose can stick its neck out and get a little air.

There's two little old ladies sitting next to him, and a few minutes later, one turns to the other and says, "You know, Myrtle, you seen one, you seen 'em all, but *this* one's eatin' my popcorn."

||||||||||||||||||||||

The teacher says to her third-grade class, "Mary had a little lamb, its fleece was white as snow,and everywhere that Mary went, the lamb was sure to go. Class, that was *poetry*, because it rhymed. If I changed the last line to 'the lamb went with her,' it would be *prose*."

She says to Dirty Johnny, "John, please give us an example of prose or poetry."

Johnny says, "Mary had a little pig, an ornery little runt...he stuck his nose between her legs, and sniffed her hairy...hey, teach, you want prose or poetry?"

The teacher says, "Prose! *Prose!*"

"...and sniffed her hairy asshole."

|||||||||||||||||||||||||

A cat comes up to the Pearly Gates.

St. Peter says, "You were a good kitty. What would you like?"

The cat says, "Just a soft blanket to spread out on."

A while later, three mice come up to the Pearly Gates.

St. Peter says, "You were good little mice. What would you like?"

The first mouse says, "We've always wanted our own skateboards."

The next day, St. Peter walks past the cat on his blanket and says, "So, you got what you wanted?"

The cat says, "Oh, yeah. And hey, the Meals on Wheels were fucking *awesome*."

|||||||||||||||||||||||||

What'd Pavlov say when the phone rang?

"Fuck! *I forgot to feed the dog.*"

|||||||||||||||||||||||||

Brezinski falls asleep on the beach and his upper legs get horribly sunburned, so he goes to the hospital.

The doctor walks in, takes a look, and says to the nurse, "Give him two Viagra now and then two every four hours."

The nurse says, "Really? Why?"

The doctor says, "It'll keep the sheets off his legs."

||||||||||||||||||||||||

Gaynes says to Mackay, "How come you never take a shower after we play golf?"

Mackay says, "Because I'm a little embarrassed. I got a small dick."

Gaynes says, "Can it still get hard twice in a row?"

Mackay says, "Sure."

Gaynes says, "How'd you like to trade it for one that looks good in the shower?"

||||||||||||||||||||||||

LaCava puts his father in a rest home. The first night during dinner his father starts to lean to the left and an attendant comes over and straightens him up. A little while later his father starts to lean to the right and the attendant runs over and straightens him up again.

Later, LaCava calls up and says, "So how is it, Pop?"

His father says, "It's not too bad, sonny boy. Today I played badminton and went in the pool. And the food's even pretty good. It's kind of nice here, but you know, sonny boy, they won't let you fart."

||||||||||||||||||||||||

Vasilas is up before a judge for killing a rare California condor.

He says, "But, your honor, I only did it to feed it to my starving family."

The judge says, "*Hmm*...well, due to the extenuating circumstances, case dismissed. Uh, my friend, before you go, just out of curiosity...what did it taste like?"

Vasilas says, "Kind of a cross between a bald eagle and a giant panda."

||||||||||||||||||||||

Dirty Johnny's walking along and a priest's coming the other way.

Johnny says, "Hey, mister, why're you wearin' your collar backwards?"

The priest says, "Because I'm a Father."

Johnny says, "Yeah? Well, my old man's got three kids and he don't wear *his* collar backwards."

The priest says, "You don't understand, son. I have *thousands* of children."

Johnny says, "You should wear your fuckin' *trousers* backwards."

||||||||||||||||||||||

McDermott gets separated from his wife in a big supermarket.

He walks up to a woman with huge jugs and says, "Could I talk to you for a few minutes?"

She says, "Okay, but why?"

McDermott says, "I can't find my wife, and anytime I start talking to a woman with tits like yours, she appears out of nowhere."

||||||||||||||||||||||

Batman runs into Superman.

He says, "Hey, Supe. What kind of day'd you have?"

Superman says, "I had a wild day. I was flying over Wonder Woman's apartment building, and she was on the roof, lying on her back with her legs spread, sunbathing naked. I had nothing to do, so I figured what the hell? I flew down and gave her a shot."

Batman says, "Boy, she must have been surprised."

Superman says, "Not as surprised as the Invisible Man."

||||||||||||||||||||||

What's a Chinese gourmet meal?
Rice and anything else.

||||||||||||||||||||||

Two old guys in a retirement home sit in the same chairs every day, and two little old ladies that live there have nothing better to do every day than to parade past and try to get them to notice. The girls put on make-up, different dresses, fix their hair, and do everything they can to get a rise out of the old guys, but the guys don't flinch. They just sit there.

One day, one of the little old ladies jumps up and says, "You know what I'm gonna do? I'm gonna *streak* 'em. That's what I'm gonna do, I'm gonna *streak* those old codgers. I'll get a rise out of 'em if it's the last thing I do."

She takes off all of her clothes and goes running in front of the two old guys.

One guy says, "W-well, what's she got on today?"

The other guy says, "I-I'm not sure. B-but it certainly needs ironing."

||||||||||||||||||||||

Mrs. Prezocki yells to her husband, "Zock, is my blinker working?"

He says, "Yes...*no*...yes...*no*..."

||||||||||||||||||||||

A lady says, "Doc, how long after my operation before I can have sex?"

He says, "You know, Ms. Quivers, you're the first person who ever asked me that before a tonsillectomy."

||||||||||||||||||||||

Melendez meets a girl in a bar and they go back to the girl's place. When they take off their clothes, she looks between his legs and he's got a really tiny pecker.

She says, "Who do you think you're gonna satisfy with *that*?"

He says, "*Me.*"

||||||||||||||||||||||

A crane's standing in a foot of water when he bends over and swallows an eel. The eel wiggles down the crane's throat, through his stomach, and out his ass. The crane bends over and swallows him again, and the eel wiggles down the crane's throat, through his stomach, and out his ass. The crane bends over and swallows him again.

As the eel's wiggling down the crane's throat, the crane bends way over, sticks his bill deep into his asshole, and says, "Loop the loop, motherfucker."

||||||||||||||||||||||

A guy says to his friend, "I can't remember if the doctor told me my wife has AIDS or Alzheimer's."

His friend says, "It's simple. Drive her to the other side of town. If she finds her way home, don't fuck her."

||||||||||||||||||||||

What's the difference between Jesus and a picture of Jesus?
It only takes one nail to hang up a picture of Jesus.

||||||||||||||||||||||

A waiter brings a lady her clam chowder and she sees his thumb is hooked over the cup.

She says, "Waiter, your thumb was in my soup."

He says, "Yeah. I got arthritis and the heat makes it feel better."

She says, "Well, why don't you stick it up your ass?"

He says, "Oh, I-I do that in the kitchen."

||||||||||||||||||||||

An old couple moves from Queens to Texas so the old guy goes out and buys himself a pair of cowboy boots.

When he gets home, he puts them on, proudly walks into the kitchen, and says to his wife, "Hey, you notice anything different about me?"

She says, "No, of course not."

He's hurt, so he leaves the room and strips naked except for the boots.

Then he walks back into the kitchen and says, "Do you notice anything different now?"

She says, "No, there's nothing different. It's hanging down today, it was hanging down yesterday, and it'll be hanging down again tomorrow."

He says, "And do you know why it's hanging down?"

She says, "No."

He says, "It's hanging down because it's looking at my new boots."

She says, "You should've bought a *hat*, Bernie, you should've bought a hat."

|||||||||||||||||||||||||||||

Two social workers pass a homeless guy who's been beaten up really badly and is lying in a gutter.

The first social worker says, "Whoever did this to him really needs help."

|||||||||||||||||||||||||||||

Warsaw Airlines Flight 101's coming in for a landing and the pilot's freaking out—the sweat's leaping off his brow.

He screeches the plane to a halt, *rrrtttt*!

He turns to the co-pilot and says, "*Man*, that's the shortest runway I ever landed on."

The co-pilot looks to the left, looks to the right, and says, "Yeah. And so *wide*."

SECTION SEVENTEEN

The Alcohol of Fame

A guy's sitting at the bar drinking when an older guy walks in. The older guy says to him, "I fuck your mother."

The older guy goes and sits down and the younger guy keeps drinking.

A few minutes later, the older guy gets up and says to the younger guy, "Your mother *sucks* my *cock*."

The bartender can't believe it's not getting a rise out of the younger guy, but he just sits there and keeps drinking.

A few minutes later the older guy gets up and says to the younger guy, "*I fuck your mother deep in her asshole*."

The younger guy says, "Pop, you're drunk. Go home."

||||||||||||||||||||||

Kelly walks into a bar and orders a beer and a shot of whiskey. The bartender serves it up, Kelly drinks the beer and pours the shot of whiskey into his shirt pocket. Kelly orders another beer and another shot of whiskey. The bartender serves it up, Kelly drinks the beer and pours the shot of whiskey into his shirt pocket.

The bartender says, "Look, Mac, I don't mean to bug you, but my curiosity is killing me. Why do you keep pouring the shots into your pocket?"

Kelly says, "It's n-none of your damn business! A-and if you be givin' me a hard time, I'll be b-breakin' yer face!"

A mouse pops his head out of Kelly's shirt pocket and says, "A-and that goes for your fuckin' cat too!"

||||||||||||||||||||||

Criblez is sitting at the bar all alone when hears, "Nice shirt."

He takes a sip from his beer and then he hears, "Nice haircut."

He calls the bartender down and says, "I thought I was alone here and somebody just said *nice haircut* and *nice shirt*. Who the hell is it?"

The bartender says, "It must be the peanuts. They're complimentary."

||||||||||||||||||||

When do you know a girl's too fat to fuck?
She pulls down her panties and her pussy's still in them.

||||||||||||||||||||

The teacher says, "Okay, class, today we're going to play a game. I want everybody to give me a sentence with the word *perhaps* in it."

Mary says, "Perhaps if we are good, the teacher won't give us any homework."

She says, "Very good, Mary."

She calls on Dirty Johnny in the back.

"John?"

Johnny says, "Yesterday, when I got home from school, my sister and her music teacher both had their pants down to their ankles. *Perhaps* they were gonna shit on the piano."

||||||||||||||||||||

What do a midget and a dwarf have in common?
Very little.

||||||||||||||||||||

A black guy goes up to the manager of a Mississippi bank and says, "I's looking for a job."

The manager says, "Well, you got some *timin'*. We got a position opening tomorrow. Forty-five thousand dollars a year and you get a car and *full benefits*."

The black guy says, "You're *jokin'*!"

The bank manager says, "Yeah, but *you* started it."

||||||||||||||||||||||

What's a homeless woman use for a vibrator?
A plastic bottle full of flies.

||||||||||||||||||||||

Rosolino says, "Doc, I think I got a tapeworm."

The doctor says, "Today's Monday. Today through Thursday, every day at noon, stick a banana and then a cookie up your ass. Then come see me at noon on Friday."

Rosolino follows the doctor's advice and then walks into his office on Friday at noon.

The doctor says, "Take off your pants and lie sideways on the table."

After Rosolino takes off his pants and lies sideways on the table, the doctor grabs his scalpel and shoves a banana up Rosolino's ass.

A few seconds later, a tapeworm sticks its head out of Rosolino's ass and says, "Where's my cookie?" and the doctor slices off the tapeworm's head with his scalpel.

||||||||||||||||||||||

Why don't men like to cuddle after sex?
Because it's like staying on the toilet when you're done taking a shit.

||||||||||||||||||||||

Two old women are in a car headed up Collins Avenue in Miami Beach.

Elsie says, "Lynnie, y-you just went through a red light."

Lynnie says, "I-I thought you were driving."

||||||||||||||||||||

Ippolito's in bed with a girl.

He says, "You're flat and you're tight."

She says, "Get off my back."

||||||||||||||||||||

How's a leper drop out of a poker game?

He throws in his hand.

||||||||||||||||||||

A little Italian guy goes into a store to buy a brassiere for his wife.

The salesman says, "What size?"

He says, "Six and-a seven-eighths."

The salesman says, "*Six and seven-eighths?* What kind of size is that?"

He says, "I measured 'em with a hat."

||||||||||||||||||||

How many Freudian psychiatrists does it take to change a light bulb?

Two. One to hold the ladder, and one to hold the penis...uh, the light bulb.

||||||||||||||||||||

A mortician's laying out the body of a man with a huge cock and he calls in his receptionist to show her.

She says, "That looks just like my Ernie's."

He says, "That big?"

She says, "No. That *dead*."

|||||||||||||||||||||||

Pinkerton's weaving down the road when a cop pulls him over.

The cop says, "Hey, pal, did you know your wife fell out a few blocks back?"

Pinkerton says, "Thank God. I thought I went deaf."

|||||||||||||||||||||||

There's a new barbershop in town and a priest goes in to get his hair cut.

When the barber's done, the priest goes to pay him, but the barber says, "No thanks, my friend. I couldn't take money from a man of the cloth."

The next day when the barber shows up at the barber shop, there's a dozen boxes of chocolates waiting for him with a thank-you note from the priest.

That afternoon a rabbi comes in, the barber cuts his hair, and when he gets done and the rabbi goes to pay him, he says, "No thanks, my friend, I couldn't take money from a man of the cloth."

The next day when he shows up at the barbershop, there's a dozen *rabbis* waiting for him.

|||||||||||||||||||||||

A girl goes up to Blair in a Las Vegas bar and says, "You want to fool around?"

Blair says, "I can't fool around with you for three reasons. The first reason is I have no money."

She says, "You can shove the other two reasons up your ass."

||||||||||||||||||||||

Behlmann meets a girl in a bar and they go back to her apartment. They go into her bedroom, and from left to right, floor to ceiling, there whole wall's full of fluffy toys. Floor to ceiling, side to side, fluffy toys, fluffy toys, fluffy toys. He fucks her.

They get done and he says, "How was I?"

She says, "Take anything from the bottom shelf."

||||||||||||||||||||||

Jesus and Moses are sitting poolside and Moses says, "I wonder if we've still got it."

Jesus says, "Why don't you see?"

Moses stands up, raises both arms, spreads them, and the pool separates into two bodies of water.

Jesus says, "That was great."

Moses says to Jesus, "Give it a shot."

Jesus gets up, starts to walk across the pool, and sinks like a stone.

He gets out and says, "I wonder what's wrong?"

Moses says, "It's probably the fucking holes in your feet."

||||||||||||||||||||||

What's more disgusting than a hickey on a hemorrhoid?
The girl who put it there.

||||||||||||||||||||||

O'Flannagan, Ravelli, and Stukowski all go for the same job, and the guy who's interviewing them's got no ears. O'Flannagan walks in first.

The guy says, "My friend, the job you're applying for requires the powers of observation. Make an observation about me."

O'Flannagan says, "Oh, but you've got no *ears*."

The guy says, "Get out of here."

Ravelli goes in next.

The guy says, "My friend, the job you're applying for requires the powers of observation. Make an observation about me."

Ravelli says, "Heh, heh, that's-a easy, Boss. You got no ears."

The guy says, "*Get out of here.*"

Ravelli goes back out to the lobby and says to Stukowski, "Ey, listen, the guy's doin' the interviewin', he's-a got no ears, and he's a *little bit-a sensitive* about it. Whatever you do, don't-a bring it up-a."

Stukowski says, "I got it."

Stukowski walks in and the guy says, "My friend, the job you're applying for requires the powers of observation. Make an observation about me."

Stukowski thinks a minute, then says, "You wear contacts."

The guy says, "You're absolutely right. Terrific observation. How could you tell?"

Stukowski says, "How could you wear *glasses*? You got no fucking *ears*."

||||||||||||||||||||||||

Leeds meets an older woman at the bar.

After a few drinks, she says, "You know, I'm fifty-seven."

He says, "Damn, you look *great* for fifty-seven."

She says, "Thanks. Hey…have you ever had the Sportsman's Double? A mother-daughter threesome?"

He says, "No. No, I haven't. A *mother-daughter threesome*? Like every guy, I wish I had, but no."

She says, "Well, tonight's your lucky night."

They have a few more drinks and then they hop in her car and she drives home.

They walk in the door, she puts on the hall light, and shouts up the stairs, "Hey, Ma, you still awake?"

||||||||||||||||||||||

An old guy with Parkinson's goes into an ice cream shop and says, "I-I want an ice cream cone."

The girl says, "What flavor?"

He says, "I-it doesn't matter, I-I'm gonna drop it anyway."

Fecalburger's standing on a train platform when the guy next to him waves and yells, "Goodbye! Your wife's a great fuck!"

After the train pulls away, Fecalburger says to the guy, "Who was that you were yelling to?"

The guy says, "My brother."

Fecalburger says, "Jesus, did I hear you right? Were you yelling, 'Your wife's a great fuck?' Are you that insensitive?"

The guy says, "As a matter of fact, I'm *very* sensitive. Truth is, my brother's wife's a *lousy* fuck, and I didn't want to hurt his feelings."

||||||||||||||||||||||

A jazz musician picks up a rich girl. He's driving her sports car ninety miles an hour as she leans over, undoes his fly, reaches in, pulls out his willie wonka, and starts playing around, fiddling, having fun. Suddenly a deer jumps in front of the car, he cuts the wheel hard to try to avoid it, loses control, the car goes down into a ditch, they roll over six or seven times, and the car finally comes to rest. When the police get there, he's still strapped to his seat.

The cops says, "Your girl was thrown from the car and killed. You sure are a lucky guy."

The musician says, "*Lucky?* Go look and see what's in her *hand*, man."

||||||||||||||||||||||

Did you hear about the gay choir boy?
He choked on his first hymn.

||||||||||||||||||||||

A girl's standing at the gates of heaven and she hears horrible screams coming from inside.

She says to St. Peter, "What's going on?"

St. Peter says, "That's the sounds of the new angels. They're getting big holes drilled in their backs for their wings and small holes drilled in their heads for their halos."

She says, "Heaven sounds *horrible*. I think I'd rather go to hell."

St. Peter says, "You can go to hell...but you'll be constantly gang-banged and sodomized."

She says, "That's okay. I've already got holes for that."

||||||||||||||||||||||

Hoffman's walking down the sidewalk, a couple's walking towards him, and Hoffman's staring at the girl very intently.

Her boyfriend says, "Have you got a *problem*, pal?"

Hoffman says, "Yeah. I want to fuck her, but I haven't got her phone number."

||||||||||||||||||||||

Rogers is standing at a bar and he keeps flirting with a girl at the other end.

Finally, she walks over and says, "You want to smell some hot pussy?"

He says, "Oh, yeah..."

She goes, "*Haahhh!*" in his face.

|||||||||||||||||||||

The receptionist calls the doctor in his office and says, "Doctor, the patient you just treated died on his way out the door. What should I do?"

The doctor says, "Turn him around so it looks like he died on the way in."

|||||||||||||||||||||

What's the difference between the fourth down and the Miss America Pageant?

On the fourth down you *kick a punt*.

|||||||||||||||||||||

A ninety-year-old woman walks into her high-rise apartment and catches her ninety-four-year-old husband in bed with another woman. When he jumps up to explain, she pushes him out onto the balcony and over the rail.

She's in court on a charge of murder and the judge says, "Do you have anything to say in your defense?"

She says, "Your honor, I figured that at ninety-four, if he could fuck, he could fly."

|||||||||||||||||||||

A guy's got a bag over his head and a gun and he goes into a sperm bank.

The receptionist says, "Th-this isn't a regular bank, i-it's a sperm bank."

He says, "I know what it is. Open that refrigerator."

She opens the refrigerator.

He says, "Take out one of those bottles."

She takes out one of the bottles.

He says, "Take off the cap."

She takes off the cap.

He says, "Now drink it down."

She drinks it. He takes the bag off of his head and it's her husband.

He says, "You *see*? It ain't so bad?"

|||||||||||||||||||||||

Beccarino's going across the desert on a camel when all of a sudden the camel stops and won't go nowhere.

A lady comes along in a jeep and says, "What's the matter?"

He says, "My camel won't go."

The lady gets down off the jeep, reaches between the camel's legs, and *bing!* The camel takes off like a shot.

Beccarino says, "What'd you do?"

She says, "I just reached between his legs and tickled his testicles a little."

He drops his drawers and says, "Well, you better tickle mine, too, 'cause I gotta catch him."

|||||||||||||||||||||||

A kid's sitting at the kitchen table.

He says, "Mom, I'm gay."

She says, "Does that mean you suck men's cocks?"

He says, "Yep."

She says, "Don't ever complain about my cooking."

||||||||||||||||||||||||

Elmer's bored so he takes off from the farm and heads for town on a rainy day. He runs into a hooker on the street and they go into an alley.

She takes it out, takes a look, and says, "It's too big."

He says, "Well, hell, that's no reason to drop it in the mud."

||||||||||||||||||||||||

How'd Helen Keller get killed crossing the road?

She stopped to read the sewer cap.

||||||||||||||||||||||||

The wife's sitting on the deck drinking a glass of wine. Her husband comes out with his newspaper, sits down, and starts to read.

She says, "I love you. I love you so much. I don't think I could make it through a day without you."

He puts down his newspaper and says, "Is that *you* talking, or is that the *wine* talking?"

She says, "It's *me* talking. To the wine."

SECTION EIGHTEEN

Tunes Equal Poon

Langione walks up to the piano player in an Italian restaurant, drops a fifty-dollar bill in his tip jar, and says, "Play 'Strangers in the Night' in 5/4 time."

The pianist says, "5/4 time? Why?"

Langione says, "Because the Godfather's going to sing it."

The piano player starts the song in 5/4 time.

The Godfather comes on stage, grabs the microphone, and starts to sing, "Strangers in the fuckin' night..."

||||||||||||||||||||||||

A guy's at a job interview.

The interviewer says, "What do you think is your biggest fault?"

The guy says, "I think my biggest fault is my honesty."

The interviewer says, "I don't think honesty is a fault."

The guy says, "I don't give a *fuck* what *you* think."

||||||||||||||||||||||||

The doctor says, "My friend, you have to stop masturbating."

The guy says, "Why, Doc?"

The doctor says, "So I can examine you."

||||||||||||||||||||||||

A drunk's doing eighty and a cop pulls him over.

The cop says, "Why're you going so fast?"

He says, "I-I wanted to get home before I p-passed out."

||||||||||||||||||||||||

A carpet layer's installing wall-to-wall carpeting in the family room of a home and he's really hungover. He finally finishes, steps back to have a look, and he sees a lump in the middle of the floor. He pats his pocket looking for a smoke and realizes his pack of cigarettes is missing. He checks his gear and coat, and when he can't find his cigarettes, he figures that's the lump. He doesn't want to rip back the carpet, and he gets an idea. He gets his hammer, walks out to the middle of the room and starts smashing the lump. It takes a while, but finally the lump is so flattened it's barely noticeable. Then he carries his tools out to the truck and there on the front seat is his pack of smokes.

As he's walking back into the house, he hears a little girl say, "Mommy, have you seen my kitten?"

||||||||||||||||||||||

Did you hear about the new *Exorcist* movie?
A lady hires the devil to get the priest out of her son.

||||||||||||||||||||||

A college kid's friends tell him they've got a girl waiting for him in his bed, but they don't tell him it's an inflatable doll.

The next day when he comes down the stairs one of the guys says, "How was your date?"

He says, "Crummy. I bit her on the ear, she farted and flew out the window."

||||||||||||||||||||||

An Italian family's sitting around the dinner table when Papa says to his oldest son, "Michael, why is it you's-a such a fat-a fuck?"

Michael says, "Papa, it's-a Mama's spaghetti. It's-a so good, I just-a eat-a so much."

Papa says, "Michael, you gotta take-a smaller bites."

He turns to his middle son and says, "Sonny, why is it you's-a such a *fat*-a *fuck*?"

Sonny says, "Papa, it's-a Mama's lasagna. My God, it's-a *so* good-a, I just *eat* it and *eat* it…"

Papa says, "Sonny, you gotta take-a smaller bites."

He says to his youngest son, "Fredo, how is it you's-a is-a always stay-a so *slim*-a and-a so *trim*-a?"

Fredo says, "It's easy, Papa. I eat lots and lots of *pussy*."

Papa says, "*Pussy*, Fredo? That's-a taste-a like *shit*."

Fredo says, "Papa, you gotta take *smaller bites*."

||||||||||||||||||||||

A woman says to a psychiatrist, "I think I'm a nymphomaniac."

He says, "I can help you. My fee's eighty dollars an hour."

She says, "How much for all night?"

||||||||||||||||||||||

A cruise ship motors past a small island and everybody on board sees a bearded man on the shore shouting and wildly waving his hands.

A passenger says, "Captain, who's that?"

The Captain says, "I have no idea. He goes nuts every year when we pass him."

||||||||||||||||||||||

What happens at a bulimic bachelor party?

The cake *jumps out of the girl.*

||||||||||||||||||||||

Schmidlap's doctor tells him he's dying of cancer.

When he gets home, he tells his son the news, and then says, "You know, I've had a good long life. Let's not be sad; let's go down to the bar and celebrate my life."

They get to the bar, right away Schmidlap starts running into his friends, and one after the other he tells them he's dying of AIDS.

On the way home, Schmidlap's son says, "Pop, you're dying of *cancer*. Why'd you tell everybody you're dying of *AIDS*?"

"Because after I'm dead, I don't want 'em fucking your mother."

|||||||||||||||||||||||

Jones goes to pick up a girl for a date, and on the way out to the car, she realizes that she has to crack a rat. She figures that she'll wait until he lets her in on her side of the car, and as he's walking around, she can fart real quick and everything will be fine.

He opens the door, she gets in, he closes the door, and as he's walking around, she lifts her leg and *whaboom!*, she really blows a hole in her parachute.

He gets in, turns, and says, "By the way, babe, I'd like you to meet the couple we're doubling with."

|||||||||||||||||||||||

Two gay guys live together and one guy gets a job. His first day of work, he comes down the stairs and there's his roommate, in the kitchen, beating off into a rubber.

He says, "What are you doing?"

His roommate says, "Packing your lunch."

|||||||||||||||||||||||

What's a platonic relationship?
A friendship between a girl and a guy who wants to fuck her.

||||||||||||||||||||||||

Walters washes up on a deserted island with Sandra Bullock. After a week of his badgering, she finally has sex with him.

Another three weeks go by, and then one day he says to her, "Would you please do me a favor? Would you put on this fake beard and moustache and walk around the island?"

Sandra agrees, puts them on, and takes off around the island.

Walters walks around the island the other way, and when he finally sees Sandra coming from the opposite direction, he runs up to her and says, "You won't be*lieve* who I'm fucking."

||||||||||||||||||||||||

A guy who can fuck thirty girls in a row gets booked on *America's Got Talent*. The night of the show, they introduce him, he walks out on stage with thirty girls, and after he fucks twenty-eight of them, he fizzles out.

The producer runs out and says, "You son-of-a-bitch, you were supposed to fuck all thirty of those girls."

The guy says, "I don't know what happened, man. Everything went fine in dress rehearsal."

||||||||||||||||||||||||

There are twin brothers who look exactly alike, but one's an incredible optimist and the other's an incredible pessimist. For their eighth birthday, the pessimist gets an expensive pen, a beautiful silk shirt, and a hundred-dollar bill. All the optimist gets is a paper bag full of horseshit.

When the pessimist is done opening up his stuff, he says, "This birthday *sucked*. This pen's probably gonna leak all over this shirt, and I'll probably *lose* the hundred-dollar bill."

The optimist looks in the bag and says, "*Whoo-hoo! A pony!* He's gone, but he'll be back!"

||||||||||||||||||||||||

An old man walks into his apartment and there's a young girl there robbing him.

He says, "I'm calling the police."

She says, "No, no, please don't. I'll do anything."

He says, "*Anything?*"

She says, "Yes, anything."

He takes off his clothes, grabs her, takes off her clothes, throws her down on the floor, and starts kissing her and feeling her tits. She grabs his cock and he starts fingering her, and then he climbs on top of her, but his dick is limp. He puts his dick in her mouth, and she sucks and sucks, but he stays limp. She licks his balls, he sticks three fingers in her ass, but his dick stays limp. She sucks his ass and he pisses all over her, he starts to chub up a bit, he quickly climbs on top of her, but right away he goes limp again.

He says, "This is *bullshit*. I'm calling the police."

||||||||||||||||||||||||||

Dirty Johnny's walking past his parents' bedroom.

He looks in and says, "I can't believe you sent me to the fuckin' psychiatrist for suckin' on my *thumb*."

||||||||||||||||||||||||

206

A group of rabbis are playing a round of golf, they're behind a very slow foursome and they keep grousing about it.

Finally their caddy says, "Fellas, the reason the foursome in front of us is so slow is they're all blind."

One of the rabbis says, "They couldn't play at *night?*"

||||||||||||||||||||||

It's World War I and a major's visiting the army hospital.

He says to the soldier in the first bed, "What's your problem, soldier?"

"Chronic syphilis, sir."

The major says, "And what are they doing for it?"

"Five minutes a day with the wire brush, sir."

The major says, "What's your ambition?"

The soldier says, "To get back to the front as soon as possible, sir."

The major says, "Good soldier," goes to the next bed and says, "What's *your* problem, soldier?"

"Chronic hemorrhoids, sir."

"And what are they doing for it?"

"Five minutes a day with the wire brush, sir."

"And what's your ambition, soldier?"

The soldier says, "To get back to the front as soon as possible, sir."

The major says, "Good man," goes to the next bed and says, "What's *your* problem, soldier?"

"Chronic gum disease, sir."

"And what are they doing for it?"

"Five minutes a day with the wire brush, sir."

The major says, "And what's your ambition?"

"To get that fucking brush before the other two, sir."

||||||||||||||||||||||

Johnson says, "Doc, I'm having trouble getting it up."

The doctor examines him and says, "The good news is I can get you back up and running. For twelve thousand dollars I can do a series of procedures that'll take a month, or for thirty thousand dollars I can do it in one operation and you'll be good as new the next day. Why don't you go home and discuss it with your wife?"

The next day Johnson walks in and the doctor says, "What'd you decide?"

He says, "We're gonna re-do the kitchen."

|||||||||||||||||||||||

How can you tell a porn star at the gas station?

Just *as the gas starts up the hose, he yanks out the nozzle and sprays the gas all over the car.*

|||||||||||||||||||||||

A farmer goes to pick up his mail-order bride. On the way home from the post office the horse pulling the wagon stops to graze.

The farmer says, "That's one, horse," whips him a few times, and the horse gets moving again.

A few minutes later the horse stops to graze again.

The farmer says, "That's *two*, horse," whips him a few times, and the horse gets moving again.

A ways down the road the horse stops to graze again.

The farmer says, "That's three, horse."

He reaches behind him, grabs his shotgun, and *boom!*, blows the horse's head off.

His new bride turns to him and says, "Wasn't that a little drastic?"

The farmer says, "That's *one*, wife."

|||||||||||||||||||||||

Hamilton wakes up in a hospital bed and says, "Doc, I can't feel my legs."

The doctor says, "That's because we amputated both of your arms."

|||||||||||||||||||||||

A little girl's walking her dog when a priest comes along and says, "Hello, little girl. What's your name?"

She says, "Rosepetal."

He says, "That's a nice name."

She says, "Yeah. When I was a little baby a rose petal fell on my head and my daddy's called me Rosepetal ever since."

The priest says, "That's so nice. Is this your doggy?"

She says, "Yeah."

The priest says, "What's his name?"

She says, "Porky."

He says, "Oh, I guess he likes to eat pork."

She says, "No. He likes to fuck pigs."

|||||||||||||||||||||||

A heart surgeon dies. At his funeral there's a huge heart covered in flowers behind the casket, and after the eulogy the heart opens and the casket rolls inside. Then the heart closes, sealing the doctor in there forever. At that point one of the mourners starts laughing his ass off.

He turns to the woman next to him and says, "I'm sorry, I was just thinking of my own funeral. I'm a gynecologist."

|||||||||||||||||||||||

Three missionaries get caught by cannibals and the cannibals throw them in a bamboo jail.

The chief pulls one of them out of the bamboo jail and says, "You have two choice...death or bunga bunga."

The missionary thinks to himself, "I don't want to die," so he says, "I'll take bunga bunga."

The chief says, "*Ugh*. Bunga bunga."

The cannibals all start jumping up and down, grunting, "Bunga bunga! *Bunga bunga!*"

They pull down his pants, bend him over a log, and they all fuck him in the ass. They throw him back in the bamboo jail, bleeding and moaning. I mean, he's got a few phone numbers, but for the most part, he's a hurtin' gherkin.

They drag out the next missionary, and the chief says, "You have two choice...death or bunga bunga."

The missionary looks back at the first guy, who's in really bad shape, but he doesn't want to die, so he says, "I'll take bunga bunga."

The chief says, "*Ugh*. Bunga bunga."

The cannibals all start jumping up and down, grunting, "Bunga bunga! *Bunga bunga!*"

Then they pull down his pants, bend him over a log, and they all fuck him in the ass. And it's a lot worse for him, because, of course, it takes the cannibals a lot longer the second time. They throw him back in the bamboo jail, yelping like a dog that's been hit by a truck, and pull out the third missionary.

The chief says, "You have two choice...death or bunga bunga."

The third missionary sees the other two guys in total agony, and says, "I couldn't handle that. I'll take death."

The chief says, "*Ugh*. Death. But first, *bunga bunga*."

About the Author

Jackie "The Joke Man" Martling is a comedian, radio personality, actor, author, and singer-songwriter. For eighteen years (1983-2001) he was Head Writer and a fixture on radio and television's *Howard Stern Show.*

In March 1979, to promote the fledgling Long Island comedy scene and the stand-up shows he was producing, he created a dirty joke line ("Use Your Finger! Dial (516) 922-WINE!") that has been in uninterrupted operation ever since.

In 1982, after founding "Governor's Comedy Shop" in Levittown on Long Island and touring as a national headliner, on a suggestion from a Washington, D.C., comedy club owner, he blindly sent his three self-produced LPs to Howard Stern upon Howard's arrival at *WNBC-AM* in New York City. Howard called him to make a guest appearance on his radio show. In 1986, Jackie became a full-time cast member and the head writer of Stern's radio and TV shows; as they say, the rest is history.

Born and raised in East Norwich, NY, a tiny hamlet on the glorious North Shore of Long Island, New York, Jackie graduated in 1966 from Oyster Bay High School and earned a degree in Mechanical Engineering from Michigan State University in 1971.

Jackie still works all around the country performing his solo act of rapid-fire jokes and his classic finale, "Stump the Joke Man."

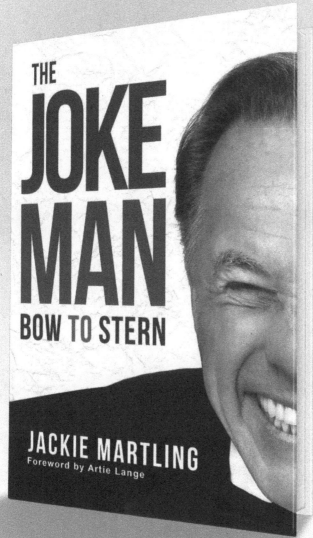

Jackie is a guest on many of the top national radio shows and podcasts. You can follow him on Twitter @JackieMartling.